MW01068933

Letters to Misty

also by misty copeland

MISTY COPELAND

with
NIKKI SHANNON SMITH

Letters to Misty

HOW TO MOVE THROUGH LIFE
WITH CONFIDENCE AND GRACE

Aladdin

NEW YORK   AMSTERDAM/ANTWERP   LONDON
TORONTO   SYDNEY/MELBOURNE   NEW DELHI

ALADDIN

An imprint of Simon & Schuster Children's Publishing Division
1230 Avenue of the Americas, New York, New York 10020
For more than 100 years, Simon & Schuster has championed authors and the stories
they create. By respecting the copyright of an author's intellectual property, you enable
Simon & Schuster and the author to continue publishing exceptional books
for years to come. We thank you for supporting the author's copyright
by purchasing an authorized edition of this book.

No amount of this book may be reproduced or stored in any format, nor
may it be uploaded to any website, database, language-learning model, or other repository,
retrieval, or artificial intelligence system without express permission. All rights reserved.
Inquiries may be directed to Simon & Schuster, 1230 Avenue of the Americas,
New York, NY 10020 or permissions@simonandschuster.com.

First Aladdin hardcover edition May 2025
Text © 2025 by Misty Copeland
Jacket illustration © 2025 by Salena Barnes
All rights reserved, including the right of reproduction in whole or in part in any form.
ALADDIN and related logo are registered trademarks of Simon & Schuster, LLC.
For information about special discounts for bulk purchases, please contact Simon & Schuster
Special Sales at 1-866-506-1949 or business@simonandschuster.com.
Simon & Schuster strongly believes in freedom of expression and stands against censorship in
all its forms. For more information, visit BooksBelong.com.
The Simon & Schuster Speakers Bureau can bring authors to your live event.
For more information or to book an event, contact the Simon & Schuster Speakers Bureau
at 1-866-248-3049 or visit our website at www.simonspeakers.com.
Jacket design by Karin Paprocki
Interior design by Mike Rosamilia
The text of this book was set in Adobe Garamond Pro.
Manufactured in the United States of America 0325 BVG
2 4 6 8 10 9 7 5 3 1
CIP data for this book is available from the Library of Congress.
ISBN 9781534443037 (hc)
ISBN 9781534443051 (ebook)

To all the dreamers, movers, and believers,
this book is for you.

To every young person searching for their path and
to those who inspire them to keep going.

Mentors, teachers, and loved ones, you are
the foundation of dreams realized.

May these letters remind you of the strength
within you, the beauty of your journey, and the endless
possibilities when you embrace who you are
with confidence and grace.

Keep striving, growing, and dancing through life.

Love,
Misty

CONTENTS

Letters to Misty

FIRST POSITION

"Attitude"—Love Yourself First

IN BALLET, *ATTITUDE* (*A-TEE-TEWD*) IS A pose where one leg is lifted and bent at a ninety-degree angle while the supporting leg remains straight. One arm is above the head, and the other is to the side.

In life, "attitude" means a settled way of thinking about someone or something, and it's typically reflected in a person's behavior. In life, try to have a positive attitude toward yourself and others.

Dear Reader,

Attitude isn't just a ballet position—it's how you carry yourself in every situation. It can shape who you are and how you feel in any moment. Over the years, I've learned the importance of keeping a positive attitude, not just toward the world around me but also toward myself.

There are times when everything feels great, and it's easy to be positive. But sometimes, things don't go as planned, and it's okay to feel a little down. What matters most is how we bounce back. We might not always be able to control what happens around us, but we can choose how we react.

When I walk into a room, I try to bring a good attitude with me, even if the environment isn't as welcoming as I'd like. I keep my eyes on my goals—joy and success—and remind myself that a positive mindset can make all the difference. It helps me stay focused and strong, no matter what challenges I face.

Remember, it's normal to have good days and bad days. What's important is finding balance and believing in yourself. Your attitude can be your superpower, helping you to move forward and achieve your dreams, one step at a time.

Here are a few things that have helped me:

Finding Joy Through Hobbies

Growing up in San Pedro, California, I found that life was often unpredictable. My family faced limited resources and constant challenges, so finding joy became essential for staying grounded. Before ballet became a central part of my life, I found happiness in simple yet meaningful activities that helped me navigate the uncertainties around me.

One of my earliest joys was journaling. I remember sitting on the floor of our small apartment with a notebook and a pen, pouring my thoughts and dreams onto the pages. Writing wasn't just a pastime; it was a way to make sense of the world around me. I could express my feelings, hopes, and fears, creating a space where I could be completely honest with myself. It became a way to see beyond my current situation and imagine a future full of possibilities where I felt confident and strong.

Music also played a significant role in finding joy. My mom loved playing music on a stereo, and I would sit close, letting the melodies fill the room. With just a bit of space to move, I would dance around our apartment, lost in the music. These moments were more than just dancing—they were an expression of emotions too big for words, an escape into a world where everything felt right.

When I discovered ballet at thirteen, it felt like an extension of these joyful moments. Ballet offered a way to channel my love for movement and expression into something structured and disciplined. But it wasn't an easy journey. Stepping into a ballet school for the first time was intimidating. I was surrounded by students who had been dancing for years, while I was just beginning. As one of the only Black girls in the school, I often felt like I didn't belong.

But even in those difficult moments, I turned to the simple joys that had always been there for me. After particularly tough rehearsals, when nothing seemed to go right, I would go home and write in my journal. Focusing on the words, reflecting on the day, and expressing myself on paper helped me reconnect with the joy that first led me to dance. These reflections reminded me that ballet, like my writing, was another form of expression—a way to process and navigate the complexities of life.

Music remained a refuge during my ballet journey. On days when I felt discouraged, I would close my bedroom door, put on my favorite album, and dance freely. These moments were about movement, not perfection. They reminded me that dance was first and foremost about joy, about the freedom to express myself without the pressures of technique and performance.

Whether you dance, write, play music, or have any other hobby, finding joy in your activities is crucial. They serve as the threads that weave through our lives, grounding us during tough times. Hobbies aren't just pastimes; they're reflections of who we are and who we're becoming.

As you grow and your passions evolve, it's important to make time for the things that make you happy. These hobbies will be there for you, just as they were for me, helping you navigate the challenges life brings. They are sources of strength, comfort, and joy, no matter what the future holds.

"Dear Misty, I love playing the piano, but sometimes life gets so busy that I don't have time for it. How do you find time for the things that make you happy, even when life gets overwhelming?"

I completely understand how overwhelming life can get, especially when you're juggling school, activities, and everything else. Even with all the demands of my career and personal life, I've found that making time for the things that bring me joy, like dance and music, is essential for my well-being.

One thing I've learned is that you don't need a lot of time to connect with what makes you happy. Even just a few minutes at the piano can be enough to recharge your spirit. It's about finding those small pockets of time in your day—maybe before school, during a break, or right before bed—when you can focus on what you love.

I also think of these joyful activities as a form of self-care. When I make time for them, I'm taking care of myself, which actually helps me handle everything else better. So instead of seeing it as one more thing to fit into your schedule, try to view it as something that supports you in all the other areas of your life.

Finally, be gentle with yourself. There will be days when it's hard to find time, and that's okay.

Keep playing, and never lose sight of what makes your heart sing.

"Dear Misty, I feel really pressured to be perfect in everything I do, including my hobbies. How can I focus on enjoying them instead of always trying to be the best?"

Believe me, I've felt the pressure to be perfect too, especially in ballet, where perfection can seem like the ultimate goal. But one of the most important lessons I've learned is that true joy and fulfillment come from the love you have for what you do, and from trying to be your best self, not from striving to outshine others.

When it comes to your hobbies, try to remember why you started them in the first place. Was it because they made you feel happy, relaxed, or inspired? Focus on that feeling instead of the outcome. Hobbies can also be a wonderful way to escape the demands of everyday life. For me, cooking has been a way to take my mind off the anxiety I sometimes feel before a performance or the stress of navigating personal challenges.

Whatever your hobby is—drawing, playing an instrument, or something else—the value lies in the experience itself. It's about the moments you spend expressing yourself, exploring your creativity, and having fun. Let your hobbies be your safe space, a way to recharge and enjoy life without the pressure of being perfect.

It's also important to give yourself permission to make mistakes. In fact, mistakes are part of learning and growing. They show that you're trying new things, pushing your boundaries, and being brave enough to be imperfect. When I look back at my own journey, it was those moments of imperfection that often taught me the most and brought me closer to my true self.

The next time you make time to enjoy your hobby, let go of the need to be perfect. Instead, focus on how it makes you feel, and let that joy be your guide. Your hobbies are meant to be a source of happiness, not stress. Embrace the freedom to explore and enjoy them just as they are.

Knowing Your Limits

Taking a break and knowing your limits is crucial in maintaining not only physical health but also mental and emotional well-being. This lesson is one that I've had to learn the hard way, and it's something I want to share with you so that you might avoid some of the pitfalls I've encountered.

During my journey as a dancer, there were countless times when I pushed myself beyond my limits, thinking that more effort would bring better results. Leading up to my first performance in New York City, I had been feeling pain in my shin for months but continued to push through because I didn't want to lose the incredible opportunity.

When I was preparing for the title role in the ballet *Firebird* at American Ballet Theatre (ABT), I was so determined to meet the choreographer's expectations that I neglected my need for rest.

The result? Six stress fractures in my tibia. I ended up needing surgery to insert a plate in my shin and spent nearly a year in recovery. That time away from the stage was incredibly challenging, but it taught me one of the most important lessons of my career: You can't pour from an empty cup. Rest is not just a luxury—it's a necessity.

This lesson applies beyond ballet. Whether you're studying for a big test, practicing for a sports event, or working on a creative project, there comes a point when rest is just as important as the effort you put in. If you don't allow yourself the time to recharge, you could risk not only injury but also losing the joy and passion that brought you to that activity in the first place.

Understanding your limits, physically and mentally, is key to long-term success. Sometimes, taking a break doesn't mean you're giving up; it means you're giving yourself the chance to come back stronger.

It's important to remember that your body and mind are your most valuable assets. I learned this firsthand during

my preparations for *Firebird*, and again after a recent surgery on my leg—though the procedure is behind me, the
pain it left behind has never fully gone away, serving as a
constant reminder of something I'll always have to manage.

When I didn't listen to my body during the *Firebird*
preparations, I learned that pushing through wasn't a sign
of strength; it was a sign of denial—denial of my injury and
the toll it was taking on my body. Taking care of yourself,
knowing when to rest, and giving your body the time it
needs to recover are the true marks of resilience.

In my experience, balancing rest with training has been
essential not just for my career but for my overall happiness.
As a young girl, I often felt like I had to constantly prove
myself, to show that I belonged in spaces where I sometimes
felt like an outsider. Through the years, I learned that being
kind to myself, allowing myself to rest, and taking breaks
didn't make me less committed; it made me smarter and
more effective in the long run.

Now, as a mother, I see the importance of this balance
even more clearly. Taking a break and caring for myself
allows me to be fully present not only in my work but also
with my family. It's a lesson that has shaped who I am as a
dancer, a woman, and a mom.

When you feel like you have to keep pushing, remember that stepping back might be exactly what you need to leap forward.

"Dear Misty, my parents expect me to always do my best and never give up. But sometimes, I feel like I need a break. How can I explain this to them?"

When I was growing up, I often felt the pressure to always give my best, whether it was in ballet or other parts of my life. It's natural to want to meet the expectations of those who care about us, especially our parents. But it's important to remember that doing your best also means taking care of yourself.

Here's how I would approach it: Start by having an open and honest conversation with your parents. Let them know that you truly value their expectations and that you want to succeed in everything you do. Then explain how sometimes the best way for you to keep doing your best is by taking a break. You can tell them that just like in sports or dance, rest is an essential part of growing stronger and performing well.

You might say something like, "Mom, Dad, I know

how much you want me to succeed, and I want that too. But sometimes, I get really tired and feel like I need a break to recharge. When I take time to rest, I can actually do better in the long run. Can we find a way to balance my work and rest so that I can keep doing my best?"

Most importantly, remember that asking for a break doesn't mean you're giving up—it means you're being smart about your limits. Your parents love you and want what's best for you, and I believe they'll understand that taking care of your well-being is just as important as working hard.

Stay strong, and always remember to listen to your body and mind.

"Dear Misty, I'm always studying hard because I want to get good grades, but sometimes I feel so tired and stressed. How do I know when it's okay to take a break from studying?"

I'm so glad you reached out to me with this question. It's wonderful that you're dedicated to your studies and want to achieve great things. But it's just as important to take care of yourself along the way.

Through my own experiences, I've learned that pushing

yourself is important but knowing when to rest is just as crucial. When you start to feel really tired and stressed, that's your body and mind telling you that it's time to take a break. It's not a sign of weakness; it's a sign that you're working hard and need to recharge to keep going.

Another good way to know when it's okay to take a break is to pay attention to how you're feeling. If you're finding it hard to concentrate, if you're feeling overwhelmed, or if you're just exhausted, that's the perfect time to step back for a little while. Even short breaks—like going for a walk, listening to some music, or just taking a few deep breaths—can make a big difference.

Think of it like dancing: You can't perform your best if you're too tired to move. The same goes for studying. Taking breaks allows you to come back to your work with a fresh mind and renewed energy, giving you a much better chance to ace your next test or do a great job on a paper.

Don't be afraid to take a pause when you need it. Your hard work will still be there when you're ready to pick it back up, and you'll be in a much better place to tackle it.

Take care of yourself, and remember, balance is key.

One of my favorite things to do particularly as a teenager and young woman in New York City was to find time to wander through Central Park. When I first moved to the city, I would spend hours there, just walking, listening to my favorite music, or writing in my journal. It became a way for me to clear my mind, reflect on my thoughts, and reconnect with myself amid the chaos of city life and the intensity of my ballet training.

It allowed me to step away from the pressures of the dance world and the expectations placed upon me. It was in these quiet moments that I could listen to my own thoughts and feelings, without any outside influences. This time alone helped me to understand myself better, to figure out what I truly wanted, and to recharge my energy.

For anyone, especially young people, spending quality time with yourself can be incredibly empowering. It's a chance to discover who you are outside school, work, or any other responsibilities. No matter if you're taking a walk, journaling, reading, building with Legos, painting or drawing, or even just lying on the floor and staring at the ceiling to let your imagination roam, these moments can help you to process your experiences, gain clarity, and find peace.

In my career, I've found that the ability to spend time alone and truly enjoy it has been a key to maintaining balance. It's allowed me to stay grounded, to avoid getting overwhelmed, and to keep my passion for dance alive. It's also taught me that it's okay to take a step back, to be with your thoughts, and to nurture your own inner world.

I encourage you to find those moments for yourself, whatever they may look like. It's not just about being alone; it's about making that time meaningful, reflective, and full of self-discovery. It's a way to build a strong relationship with yourself, one that will support you in all areas of your life.

"Dear Misty, people always ask me what I want to be when I grow up, and honestly, I don't have a clue. It feels like I don't even know myself well enough to decide, and it's embarrassing when I can't give an answer. How can I start to figure out who I am and what I really want?"

This can be so hard, especially when life feels overwhelming or full of distractions. Growing up, I faced similar struggles, and it wasn't always easy to carve out the time or space to truly get to know myself. But I can tell you that spending time alone became one of the most important practices in my life—it's how I learned to listen to my own thoughts, understand my desires, and really figure out who I was beyond the roles and expectations others placed on me.

A lot of that time alone was spent journaling. It became an essential tool for self-discovery and understanding my own journey. In the quiet moments alone with my journal, I found a safe space to express myself freely and explore different aspects of my inner world.

Most often, I used my journal like a diary. I wrote about my daily experiences, detailed my emotions, and reflected on the interactions I had each day. This helped me process my feelings and track my personal growth over time.

To start connecting with yourself, try setting aside some time each day—no matter how small—to be alone with your thoughts. It doesn't have to be elaborate. Simply sitting quietly in your room can be just as effective as journaling or any other practice you might use to reflect. The key is to allow yourself the space to be with your own thoughts and feelings, without judgment or distraction.

Remember, this is a process, and it may take some time to feel comfortable being alone. But the more you practice, the more you'll discover about yourself. You'll start to notice patterns in your thoughts, identify what truly excites you, and understand what might be holding you back. This self-awareness is a powerful tool, one that will guide you as you navigate your journey.

So take that first step, give yourself the time and space you deserve, and know that connecting with yourself is an ongoing practice—one that will help you understand and appreciate the incredible person you are.

"Dear Misty, I get bored when I'm alone and don't know how to enjoy spending time by myself. How did you learn to love your alone time?"

Learning to enjoy being alone is tough, and honestly, it's one of the hardest things to do in life. Being still—on your own, with others, or even onstage—is a skill you have to build and hone over time. It's something I've had to work on a lot throughout my career.

Growing up, I was always a bit of a loner, even though I had five siblings. I spent a lot of time alone, and it wasn't always comfortable. It's easy to feel bored or restless when you're by yourself because we're so used to constant movement and distraction. But being alone can also give you the time and space to really listen to yourself—to figure out what you want and how you feel.

For me, the key was realizing that alone time didn't have to be filled with activities. Sometimes, just being still, sitting quietly, or reflecting is enough. It's okay to feel uncomfortable at first—it's part of the process. You'll find that being alone helps you recharge and stay connected to yourself in ways that are harder to do when you're always surrounded by people.

Think of it like practicing a new skill. The more you allow yourself to sit with those quiet moments, the easier and more rewarding it becomes. No matter if you're daydreaming while playing, sitting outside, or just enjoying the silence, it's worth it to get comfortable with your own company. Trust me, it will make a big difference in how you connect with yourself and the world around you.

Rooting for Yourself

Rooting for yourself is one of the most important things you can do in life, no matter what your dreams or goals are. This idea is something that I had to embrace fully throughout my career, especially during the most challenging times.

I've been fortunate to have had incredible support from

teachers, mentors, and friends throughout my journey as a dancer. But there came a point when I realized that, as much as others might believe in me, it was essential that I believe in myself.

One of the most pivotal moments in my career came when I was offered a position with Dance Theatre of Harlem, a prestigious company where I would have been surrounded by dancers who look like me. It was tempting, and it would have been a comfortable choice. But deep down, I knew that my dream was to dance for ABT and to move up the ranks within that company. Turning down that opportunity was a difficult decision, but it was a moment where I had to root for myself and believe in my vision for my future. If I hadn't stood firm in that belief, I don't know where I would be today.

That said, being the only Black woman at ABT for the first ten years of my career was incredibly tough. There were days when I questioned if I belonged, if I should continue in a place where I felt so different. The pressure was immense, and the feeling of being alone was something I struggled with constantly. But I came to realize that if I didn't present myself with confidence—if I didn't act like I belonged— then how could I expect anyone else to see me that way?

Rooting for yourself means having the courage to stay aligned with your goals, despite the challenges or when the odds seem stacked against you. It means believing in your worth and your right to pursue your dreams, no matter how daunting the journey might be. For me, this mindset has been crucial in navigating the challenges of my career. It's what helped me push through barriers, both external and internal, and it's what continues to drive me today.

No matter if you're facing challenges in school, trying to achieve a goal, or just figuring out who you are, remember that you have to be your own biggest fan. Your confidence in yourself will not only help you overcome obstacles but also inspire others to see your potential and support you along the way.

> "Dear Misty, I've been told that I won't make it as a veterinarian because I'm too sensitive, and it's hard not to let that get to me. How do you block out negativity and keep believing in yourself?"

I know it feels tough when people doubt what you can do, especially when you care about your dreams so much. I've been there too. When I was starting out in ballet, some people told me I wouldn't make it because of how I looked and because I started training later than most dancers. It was really hard to hear.

But one important thing I learned is that sometimes people's doubts are about their own limits, not yours. Your sensitivity is actually a great strength, especially for a career as a veterinarian, where caring deeply is so important. It means you'll be great at understanding and helping animals.

Whenever you hear something negative, try to remember why you started dreaming of your career in the first place. Write down your dreams and the good things about yourself and read them when you feel down. Here's something you might write: *I am caring and smart. My sensitivity is my strength. Every day, I'm getting closer to my dream.*

Also, find people who believe in you—like family, friends, or teachers. Their support can make a big difference when you're feeling unsure. And don't forget to be your own biggest cheerleader! Celebrate your small successes along the way, like doing well on a test or helping an animal. These moments are important and show how much you're growing.

Remember, every great dream starts with a dreamer just like you. Keep believing in yourself, keep working hard, and don't let anyone else's doubts stop you from achieving your goals.

"Dear Misty, I sometimes feel like I have to change who I am to be accepted by my friends. How can I stay true to myself and not doubt my worth?"

When I was fifteen, I went to a sleepover with some ballet friends. It was meant to be an innocent night, but a few of the girls, who were older and seemed so much more adventurous than I was, decided we should all get into a boy's car.

I remember not wanting to go—I wasn't the type of teenager who went to parties or did anything like that. But I didn't want to seem different or be the only one saying no, so I got in the car with them. It was dark, and the boy was driving recklessly down winding hills. I was terrified the entire time. Nothing bad happened that night, but I felt like I had let myself down because I knew better.

That experience taught me a lot about staying grounded in who I am. I realized that being accepted by others isn't worth compromising your values or doing something that makes you feel uncomfortable. It's okay to say no—it doesn't make you less cool or less of a friend. In fact, standing up for what feels right to you shows real strength.

Remember, your worth isn't tied to what other people think of you. It comes from being confident in who you are and honoring your values. Surround yourself with people who accept and celebrate the real you. Those are the friends who truly matter.

Believing in yourself is one challenge, but celebrating yourself—really taking the time to acknowledge your own successes—can be even harder. I've always found it difficult to walk the line between confidence and arrogance. When I was younger, I often confused the two and worried that celebrating my achievements would come off as bragging. But over the course of my career, I've come to realize that it's not only okay to celebrate your wins but essential.

In the world of ballet, where every performance is scrutinized, it's easy to get caught up in what went wrong or what could have been better. But when you don't take the time to recognize your own progress and the milestones you've reached, it becomes so much harder to keep going. Early in my career, I was so focused on what I hadn't yet achieved that I forgot to appreciate how far I'd come.

For a decade, I was the sole Black woman at American

Ballet Theatre, which brought its own unique challenges and pressures. Throughout that time, I was hyperfocused on reaching the next level, constantly pushing myself toward the next role or opportunity. It wasn't until I achieved a significant milestone in my career—my promotion to principal dancer—that I truly understood the importance of pausing to celebrate my achievements.

When I received the news of my promotion, it wasn't met with fanfare or an extravagant celebration. In fact, I had dinner plans with friends that night, and when my husband asked if I wanted to cancel to do something special, I insisted we keep the plans. Celebrating with the people who had supported me throughout my journey, who understood the dedication and hard work it took, was exactly how I wanted to mark the occasion. It was a reminder that the joy of achievement is best shared with those who have been by your side.

Equally important are the smaller victories, the ones that might seem insignificant in the grand scheme but are monumental in their own right. For example, there was one day I had a really tough rehearsal. I woke up feeling super stiff and tired, in both my body and my mind. Knowing what I could handle, I took some extra time to warm up slowly and set my own pace for the day. Making it through that rehearsal without being hard on myself or comparing my progress to other days felt like a small victory. Not only that, it taught me a big lesson about the importance of being patient and taking care of myself. It was a reminder that listening to what you need is a key part of doing your best.

Both these moments—celebrating my promotion in a simple, meaningful way, and acknowledging the triumph of getting through a tough rehearsal day—have taught me the importance of being my own biggest fan. No one knows the work and sacrifice you put in better than you do. Learning to celebrate your own successes, big and small, is not just about giving yourself a pat on the back; it's about recognizing your growth, your resilience, and the incremental steps you take each day toward your goals.

You deserve to acknowledge your hard work and to feel proud of what you've accomplished.

"Dear Misty, what do you do to remind yourself of your achievements when you start to doubt your abilities?"

Doubt can be a familiar visitor for anyone striving to achieve great things, myself included. When I begin to question my abilities, I have a special way of reminding myself of all I've accomplished, which might help you, too.

Instead of seeking validation through external opinions, I turn to something far more personal and uplifting: kind notes and messages I've received from friends, family, and mentors. After each performance, award, or any significant milestone, I save the congratulations and supportive messages I receive. These are not just words; they are affirmations of my hard work and talent from the people who truly know and support me.

Whenever doubt creeps in, I revisit these messages. Reading them allows me to relive the moments of success and the positive impact I've made on others. It's a powerful reminder that my journey is valued and that my achievements are real and recognized by those who matter most to me.

Keeping a "success journal" filled with these notes, along with my own reflections on achievements and milestones, reinforces my confidence. It's a tangible testament to my journey, filled with love and support, that helps drown out any negative voices, including my own sometimes.

So gather those kind notes; maybe even make a scrapbook or a digital folder. When you feel unsure, flip through it and let the positive energy lift you up. Remember, your accomplishments are significant, and your journey is uniquely yours. Trust in the love and support of your circle, and keep pushing forward, one step at a time.

"Dear Misty, how important is it to have friends and family who celebrate with you? What if my family doesn't really understand why my goals are a big deal?"

It's true that not everyone will fully understand the intricacies of the paths we choose, especially in fields like dance, which can seem like a world of its own. My family, not being from the dance world, often didn't grasp the details of my journey or what committing to ballet entailed. However, they supported the aspects they could relate to and understand.

For example, they knew I was an introvert—so shy that even reading aloud in class was a struggle for me. They saw the courage it took for me to step onto a stage and perform in front of thousands, and they celebrated that growth. Sharing this perspective with me helped them connect with my experiences in their own way, appreciating the personal milestones that were part of my dance career.

If your family doesn't understand the significance of your goals right now, try breaking things down in ways that relate to their experiences or values. Help them see your achievements through the lens of personal growth or resilience—something that they can appreciate. Even if they never fully understand every aspect of your journey, their support in the areas they do grasp can be just as meaningful.

Remember, the support of friends and family doesn't always need to come from a place of full understanding. It often comes from seeing your dedication and growth, and from wanting to see you succeed, no matter the arena. Keep sharing your successes and challenges with them, and celebrate every step forward, knowing that their support is rooted in their love and respect for you.

creating your own sense of belonging

As a young girl, I was introverted, and a lot of that came from feeling ashamed and embarrassed about my life. My family spent most of my childhood houseless, living in and out of motels and constantly moving, which made it hard for me to connect with others. I didn't want people to know about my situation, so I kept to myself, blending into the background as much as possible. I really struggled to find where I fit in.

But when I discovered dance, everything changed. Dance became my form of freedom and expression, and I realized that my introversion wasn't because I didn't want to be seen—it was because I needed to be seen in a way that felt right for me. Onstage, I could be powerful, graceful, and strong, communicating in a way that words never allowed me to. Dance gave me a voice.

However, as I immersed myself in the world of ballet, I encountered a new challenge: fitting in while staying authentic to myself. Ballet, with its long history and strict traditions, often demanded conformity. The message was clear: To be a successful ballet dancer, you needed to blend in, to move as one with the corps de ballet, and to fit a very specific mold. For someone like me, who was just beginning to discover who I was and who I wanted to be, this felt like an impossible contradiction.

I had finally found my voice, yet I was being told that to succeed, I had to silence parts of myself again. It was an internal struggle—balancing my individuality with the demands of an art form that seemed to require me to give it up. But what I realized over time is that unison and fluidity in dance don't have to mean losing your individuality.

In fact, it's your unique qualities that can bring something new and valuable to the art. Being one of the few Black women in a predominantly white profession, my late start in ballet at thirteen, and my athletic build all presented unique challenges but also opportunities to enrich the art form. My presence in roles like the Firebird showcased not just the power of diversity but the beauty that different perspectives bring to traditional narratives. By embracing these aspects of my identity and demonstrating excellence onstage, I both found my place and broadened the perceptions of what fitting in can mean in ballet. And this is important not just for dance but for life: Fitting in doesn't mean losing yourself. It means finding your place and showing that your unique voice has value.

"Dear Misty, I'm always trying to make everyone happy, but I feel like I'm losing myself in the process. How can I start standing up for what I want without feeling like I'm letting people down?"

I've felt exactly the way you're feeling, both when I was a little girl and even during my early ballet career. I had a really hard time standing up for myself or saying what I truly felt because I was so worried about disappointing others or not living up to their expectations. Instead of speaking up, I often stayed quiet, and that led to me feeling more isolated, like no one really knew who I was or what I needed.

Then I realized that standing up for myself and expressing how I felt didn't push people away—it actually brought them closer. By sharing my thoughts and being honest about my feelings, I found that people understood me better, and I felt more connected. It gave me a sense of power and control over my own journey. And that's something I want you to know: When you stay connected to who you are, everyone wins. You show the world who you really are, and that allows others to truly see and support you in the ways that matter.

I encourage you to start by listening to what *you* need. Don't be afraid to share that with the people around you. It might feel scary at first, but as you gain more experience, you'll realize how important it is to voice what you need. It will strengthen your relationships and, most importantly, help you stay in tune with yourself. Standing up for yourself isn't about letting others down—it's about lifting yourself up.

"Dear Misty, I just moved to a new school, and I feel out of place. Everyone already has their friend groups, and I'm shy. What advice do you have for

someone who's struggling to fit in while still being
themselves?"

Before I was seven years old, I attended about five different schools because my family was constantly moving. It was hard to settle in, make friends, or feel like I belonged anywhere. So I absolutely understand what it's like to feel out of place, especially when everyone else seems to have their groups already formed.

Through my experience, I've come to realize that it's okay to take your time. You don't have to fit in right away or change who you are just to make friends. For me, dance became the way I connected with others, especially during times when I didn't have the words to say how I was feeling. It gave me a place where I could express myself and feel seen for who I truly was.

Start by looking for things you enjoy doing—such as a hobby, a class, or an activity that brings you joy. Often, those spaces will naturally lead you to people who share similar interests, and you'll feel more comfortable connecting with them. It doesn't have to happen all at once—sometimes small steps, like saying hi or asking someone about their day, can make a big difference over time.

The most important thing is to honor who you are. You don't need to change to fit in, and the right people will appreciate you for being you. Be patient, and remember that finding your place will come. I know it's not easy, but staying grounded in yourself is always the best way to build real, meaningful connections.

Belonging, for me, has always been about finding common ground with those around me rather than focusing on what makes us different. As a young professional dancer, I often felt like I didn't belong. Sometimes, that feeling was reinforced by subtle gestures or outright comments that made it clear I wasn't what others expected. But I didn't let that push me away. Instead, I sought mentorship and advice from people I trusted, people with more experience, who helped me navigate these challenges. They showed me that belonging isn't just about waiting for others to accept you; it's about finding ways to connect with people, even in environments where you feel like the "only."

At first, I struggled with the tension: I had finally found my voice, but ballet seemed to require me to suppress what made me unique. Over time, I realized that embracing my individuality didn't mean rejecting ballet—it meant redefining what belonging could look like within it. I began to understand that by accepting my differences and staying true to my experiences, I could bring something new to the art, creating my own sense of belonging without having to conform.

This lesson became even more important as I moved up the ranks at American Ballet Theatre. I didn't initially realize that I might become the first Black woman to be promoted to principal dancer. But as I began to understand the weight of that responsibility, I saw that being the first wasn't just about me—it was about opening doors for others and expanding the idea of what belonging in ballet could mean.

Being the first could have felt isolating, but instead, I chose to turn that experience into one of pride and purpose. I leaned on the advice of mentors who helped me understand that being the first is not a burden but a unique opportunity to pave the way for others. By embracing both my individuality and my role as a trailblazer, I found that I could fit into the world of ballet in a way that was authentic to who I was.

Belonging isn't about losing yourself to fit in—it's about bringing your full self into every space you enter. Regardless of whether you're the first, the only, or simply someone who feels different, you have the power to create your own sense of belonging by accepting what makes you unique and finding ways to connect with those around you. When you allow yourself to be seen, others can learn from your journey, and you help create a space where everyone feels they belong.

> *"Hey Misty, I'm usually the only Black rider at my horse shows, and it's tough when people stare at me like I don't belong. How do you handle being the only Black dancer in the room?"*

It can feel isolating to be the only one who looks like you in a space, especially when you're met with stares that make you feel like you don't belong. I've been in that position throughout my career as a dancer, where I was often the only Black woman in the room. That feeling of being different can be really tough, but I want you to remember something important—you absolutely *do* belong.

When I felt like people were staring at me or making me feel out of place, I reminded myself that I had worked just as hard as anyone else to be there. I deserved my spot, and so do you. I focused on why I was there in the first place—because of my love for ballet and my passion for performing. For you, it's your love of riding and being at those horse shows. Don't let other people's looks or opinions take that away from you. Use those moments to fuel your drive and remind yourself that you're breaking barriers just by being there.

Remember that your presence is powerful. Every time you show up, you're paving the way for others who will come after you, just like I did in ballet. You're showing the world that we all deserve to be in these spaces, no matter how unfamiliar it may seem to others.

Keep your head high, stay focused on your passion, and know that you belong just as much as anyone else.

"HI MISTY, I'm new at school, and I haven't made any friends yet. I'm pretty shy, and some kids make fun of me for it. HOW did you deal with people who weren't nice to you?"

I was very shy growing up too, so much so that my nickname was "Mouse" because I hardly spoke. It wasn't easy, and I know how hurtful it can be when people don't understand you and make fun of your quietness. I realized that being shy also had its strengths. It allowed me to observe the people around me, understand my environment, and take my time in building friendships.

One important lesson I've gained is that the right people—the ones who truly see and appreciate you for who you are—will find you in time. And when they do, it will be so worth it. You don't have to rush or change yourself to fit in. Be who you are, and trust that those friendships will come.

When I was younger, dance became my way of expressing myself without words. It gave me confidence and helped me feel like I had a voice, even in moments when I wasn't speaking. If there's something you love to do, focus on that and let it be your strength. You'll find that when you're doing what you love, people who value and understand you will naturally be drawn to you.

As for the kids who aren't being nice, remember that their words don't define you. Sometimes people pick on others because they don't understand them, or they're dealing with their own insecurities. Be patient and know that your true friends—the ones who value the real you—are out there, and they will find you.

Letting Go of People: Navigating Change

Change is a constant in life, and while it can be intimidating, it's also one of the greatest opportunities for growth.

Moving to a new place, evolving in your career, or realizing that a friendship no longer serves you—change is something you can welcome, and it is essential for becoming the person you're meant to be.

In my journey, I've faced many significant changes—both in my personal life and in my career. Each one came with its own challenges, but every time I accepted those changes, I found myself growing in ways I never imagined. One of the most difficult aspects of change can be letting go of people or situations that no longer serve you. It's natural to hold on to the familiar, even though you know deep down that it's time to move on. But letting go doesn't mean failure; it means making room for new opportunities and people who are aligned with who you are becoming.

Change isn't just about what happens around you; sometimes, the biggest changes happen inside you. There have been many times in my life when I had to let go of old habits or ways of thinking to become a better version of myself. As I grew up, I thought not just about the person I wanted to be but also about the dancer I was becoming. Being an artist means you can't stay the same forever—you have to keep changing and growing. It's not always easy.

It takes courage, thinking carefully about what works, and being willing to try new things.

Every time I've gotten hurt, I've had to stop and think about how I can come back stronger. I've learned to change the way I train and take care of my body so I don't make the same mistakes. These changes haven't always been comfortable, but they've helped me grow.

One of the hardest things I've done was go onstage while feeling extremely vulnerable. There were moments when I didn't feel like I was at my best, but I knew that to grow, I had to push through the discomfort and those challenging moments. I learned that being vulnerable is actually a strength, not a weakness. It's in these challenging times that you find out what you're truly capable of.

I want to encourage you to be okay with change, even if it feels scary. If you're moving to a new school, dealing with a shift in your friendships, or just feeling different from who you used to be, know that change is a natural part of life. It's okay to feel uncertain, but remember that every change brings new opportunities to grow, learn, and discover more about yourself.

If you find yourself needing to let go of a relationship or situation that no longer serves you, trust that you're making space for something better. Letting go can be difficult, but it's a necessary part of evolving into the person you're meant to be. Allow yourself to grow, and don't be afraid to shed old habits, beliefs, or relationships that are holding you back.

Lastly, be patient with yourself as you navigate these changes. Growth takes time, and it's okay if it doesn't happen overnight. Surround yourself with people who support your growth, and remember that every step forward, no matter how small, is progress.

So the next time you face change, whether it's within yourself or in your surroundings, approach it with an open heart. It will lead you to new and beautiful places in your life. And always remember that change is not something to fear but an opportunity to become the best version of yourself.

> "Hey Misty, I've been best friends with someone since first grade, but now we're growing apart. It feels weird, and I don't know how to deal with it. Have you ever had to let go of a friendship?"

It can be confusing when you start to grow apart from someone who has been a big part of your life. I've gone through this too. I've had friendships that faded when life took us in different directions, and sometimes we found our way back to each other after some time apart. As we grow and change, our friendships might go through seasons. Time, life experiences, and maturity can help bring people back together when the connection is still there.

But I've also had friendships that didn't recover. Sometimes, when the effort to maintain the relationship isn't mutual or one person is hurt too deeply, it can be hard to find your way back. And that's okay too. Letting go of a friendship doesn't take away the value of what you shared; it makes space for both of you to grow in the ways you need to.

What matters most is being honest with yourself and recognizing when a friendship is no longer serving you or them in a healthy way. If that happens, it's okay to let go and allow both of you the room to move in different directions. It doesn't mean the friendship wasn't important or meaningful—it just means that sometimes, people grow apart, and that's part of life's journey.

"Dear Misty, I'm scared of making changes in my life because I'm worried about failing. Have you ever been afraid of failure when going through big changes, and how did you push through it?"

I totally understand how scary change can be. For me, change has always been unsettling because it throws off the stability I've craved and didn't always have growing up. I've found that stability is something I need too, so when change comes along, it can feel overwhelming. But at different stages in my life, I've had to embrace change to make my career and my life healthier. One of the biggest shifts I had to make was changing the way I trained for ballet as my career progressed. It was terrifying because I didn't know if it would work, but I knew that staying the same wasn't an option if I wanted to grow.

The thing about change is that it's a risk—but it's a risk worth taking. If you don't try, you won't grow, and if you're not happy where you are, staying the same will only make things harder in the long run.

I encourage you to question what failure really means. Who defines it? Sometimes, what we see as failure is actually just a step toward something beautiful. What feels like a setback can be part of the process that leads to growth and positive change. I've learned that even if something doesn't go the way I hoped, it doesn't mean I've failed—it just means I'm on the way to something new.

So if you're scared of making changes, that's okay! Just

know that with every step, you're getting closer to the growth that you need. Embrace it, trust the process, and remember that every risk can lead to something better.

Feeling Othered: Turning Pain into Strength

When I was younger, I was often teased for being different. I was small with petite features and really big feet. I never felt like I fit the standard of beauty that the kids around me believed in. Their teasing made me feel less than, and I carried that sense of inadequacy with me. I didn't feel beautiful because I didn't fit into what others saw as beautiful.

But when I started ballet, everything changed. The very things I was teased about—my long limbs, big feet, and small head—became my superpower in the ballet world. In ballet, these physical attributes were considered assets. My long limbs allowed me to create beautiful lines, and my feet became a source of strength and balance. Suddenly, I was in a world where my differences were celebrated rather than ridiculed.

Yet, it wasn't just the acceptance in ballet that made me feel beautiful; it was the confidence that grew from finally feeling like I belonged somewhere. This acceptance allowed me to embrace my unique qualities and find beauty in what made me different. I realized that the very things that made me feel othered were the things that made me special.

It has taken me many years and countless experiences to truly understand this. I've learned to own who I am and to find strength in my uniqueness rather than seeking everyone's acceptance and approval.

Embrace what makes you different. It's those very differences that can become your greatest strengths. Don't let others' opinions shape how you see yourself. Instead, let your uniqueness shine, and remember that true confidence and beauty come from within. The things that make you feel othered today might just be the things that make you extraordinary tomorrow.

> "Dear Misty, I love video games and coding, but the kids at my school think that's weird. How can I be proud of what I love without worrying about what others think?"

I was never the "cool kid" in school either. Maybe it was because of how I looked, where I lived, or how poor my family was, but I often felt like I didn't fit in. I was also called "weird" sometimes, just because I didn't look or act like everyone else. But I've learned over time that being different—whether it's how you look, where you come from, or what you love—doesn't mean something's wrong with you. In fact, those differences are what make you stand out.

It's not easy when others don't understand or appreciate your passions, but remember, being unique isn't a bad thing. You don't have to fit into anyone else's idea of what's "cool" or "normal." If you're passionate about video games and coding, that's something to be proud of. Passion gives you strength and motivation, and when you focus on what you love, it helps you rise above the opinions of others.

When I faced teasing or felt out of place, I kept reminding myself why I loved ballet and why it made me happy. That passion gave me the strength to keep going, and over time, I found people who appreciated me for who I was. The more I embraced my uniqueness, the less I cared about what others thought. And eventually, those things that made me "weird" became my strengths.

Keep doing what you love, and don't be afraid to be different! Surround yourself with people who support you and remember that it's okay if not everyone gets it. As long as you're proud of who you are and what you love, that's what matters most.

"Dear Misty, I have a stutter, and people sometimes make fun of how I talk. Did you ever feel like people focused on your differences, and if so, how did you overcome that?"

A dear friend and mentor once told me that standing out for my differences—especially for things beyond my control—could be my greatest strength. That advice changed the way I saw myself. Instead of feeling like my differences held me back, I began to see them as opportunities to show resilience and inspire others.

For you, having a stutter might feel like an obstacle right now, but it's also a reminder of your courage. Every time you speak, you're showing strength, determination, and the power of your voice. Your voice matters, and it deserves to be heard—stutter and all.

When people focused on my differences, like my body type or background, it wasn't easy. But I learned to channel that focus into something positive by embracing what made me unique. By doing so, I not only grew stronger but also showed others what was possible.

If you can shift your perspective and see your stutter as part of what makes you strong, you'll be unstoppable. Surround yourself with people who lift you up, and focus on the areas where you feel happy and proud of who you are. Your resilience has the power to inspire others who may feel like their differences set them apart too. You're not just standing out—you're standing strong.

SECOND POSITION

"Développé"—discover yourself

IN BALLET, A *DÉVELOPPÉ* (*DAYV–LAW–PAY*) is a movement where the working leg is drawn up to the knee of the supporting leg and then extended into the air with control and grace. In life, we are also developing— growing into who we are meant to be.

Just as a *développé* unfolds, discovering yourself is about taking what you've learned and slowly revealing your unique self to the world. It requires patience, balance, and courage. As you move forward, you'll learn to carry yourself with confidence and authenticity, becoming stronger with each step.

Dear Reader,

A développé *in ballet is all about control and strength. Just like the leg extending outward in the movement, our own personal development takes time and effort, growing gradually as we learn more about ourselves and the world around us. Every stretch, every challenge, is part of that growth.*

If someone had told the younger me that I'd become the first Black female principal ballerina at American Ballet Theatre, I might not have believed them. My family struggled—moving often and sometimes unsure of where our next meal would come from. But we had love, music, creativity, and laughter, which helped me grow despite the challenges. I found movement, I found dance, and eventually, ballet found me. Each step along the way became part of my own personal développé.

Ballet gave me the discipline and consistency to keep moving forward, but it also gave me the freedom to explore and express myself, shaping who I am today—not just as a dancer, but as a person.

Remember, like the développé, *growth doesn't*

happen all at once. Each stage is important, and it's okay to take your time, to build your strength before extending yourself fully. Every experience, no matter how easy or difficult, helps you become who you are becoming.

In this section, I've shared some of my stories and advice to guide you as you continue your own development. Just like in ballet, growth in life comes with patience, practice, and persistence. Trust in your journey, and remember that despite how slow growth may seem, you are always moving forward with grace.

Finding People Who Let Me Be Myself (Besties!)

Growing up, we all want to find that one friend—or group of friends—who lets us be our truest selves. For me, that friend was Catalina. She was my first really close friend. I met her on my first day at a formal ballet studio, which was a huge step from practicing at the Boys & Girls Club on the basketball courts. I was nervous walking into that studio for the first time, unsure of how I'd fit in.

Then I walked into the dressing room, and there was

Catalina. She turned to me with this incredible confidence and asked, "Oh hi! How old are you?" She said it with such joy, like she was already the queen of the ballet studio. I remember thinking she must have been much older, but when I answered, "I'm thirteen," she proudly told me she was only ten! Her energy was larger than life, and from that moment, I knew we'd be friends.

Before Catalina, my world revolved around my siblings. After school, I'd head straight home, never venturing out with friends. But Catalina brought a spark into my life, pushing me to embrace adventures I never thought I'd take on. That spirit carried us through years of friendship filled with laughter, tears, and growth. I can still smell the smoky bonfire on my hoodie from our Saturday nights after ballet class—teenagers running along the beach, swapping scary and silly stories, and blasting boy-band anthems. Those moments not only defined my middle and high school years but also showed me what true friendship could look like—a mix of joy, discovery, and belonging.

As someone who didn't—and still doesn't—have a large group of friends, I've always been able to easily recognize that safety in friendships is key. Some friendships I've had didn't feel safe enough to open up in, and because of that, they didn't last or just stayed surface-level. But with Catalina, I could always be myself.

One thing I've learned is that being similar to someone doesn't always make a friendship work. In fact, many of my lasting friendships have been with people who were different from me, who challenged me in new ways. What made those friendships strong was that we shared common loves, passions, and interests, even though our personalities weren't the same. That connection is what creates a lasting bond—when you can be different and still find joy in what you share.

Catalina was that friend for me, someone who made me feel seen and supported. Because of those experiences with her, I was open and ready when I met my adult best friend, Leyla, at seventeen in New York City. I knew how beautiful and important friendship could be, and I was ready to receive hers.

If you haven't found your "people" yet, don't worry—they're out there. It can take time, but stay true to yourself and keep following your passions. Friendships often grow when you least expect them. When you do find those friends, it will feel natural, and they'll accept you for who you are.

"Dear Misty, I have a bunch of friends in my class, but I don't have a best friend. I don't really trust very

many people, because there is a lot of gossip at my
school. How can I tell who my true friends are?"

I understand how hard it can be to find someone you truly
trust, especially when there's a lot of gossip around. It's wonderful that you have a group of friends, but I know it can
feel different when you're searching for that one person you
can really count on.

From my experience, true friendship isn't just about being
comfortable around each other; it's about feeling supported
and accepted for who you really are. I've had friendships where
I felt I had to hold back or wear a mask to fit in, and those relationships never went beyond the surface. On the other hand,
I've also had friendships where I could be myself without hesi-
tation, where we were able to be open and real with each other.
Those are the relationships that have truly shaped my life.

A true friend is someone who wants the best for you, who
listens, supports, and respects you. They won't talk behind
your back or spread rumors. You won't have to pretend to be
someone else around them, and they'll make you feel comfortable just being yourself. While sharing common interests
can bring you closer, the most important part of a real friendship is the care, trust, and love you show for each other.

It's also important to remember that friendships can grow and change. Just like you, other people are learning and growing too. A misunderstanding or mistake doesn't always mean a friendship is over. Sometimes, with time, those bonds can become even stronger.

Don't rush to find that person you trust completely—it's okay if it takes a while. You don't need a huge group of best friends; even one person who truly values you is enough. Pay attention to how people make you feel—and notice where you feel safe, valued, and respected. If you feel that way around someone, it's a good sign they're a true friend.

Trust your instincts, and remember that friendships are part of life's journey and your growth.

"Dear Misty, my best friend in the whole world just told me he doesn't want to be friends anymore. I still want to be his friend, but my mom said I'm better off without him. What would you do?"

It's so hard when someone you care about decides they don't want to be friends anymore, especially when you still want to be. I know it can feel confusing and hurtful, and it's okay to feel sad about it.

I've had really close and beautiful friendships end too. One of my close adult friends went away for many years, and we lost touch. But later, we reconnected when we were both in a place where we could accept each other for who we were and where we were in life. Friendships can change, and sometimes they come back even stronger. However, there have been times when holding on to a relationship caused more harm than good. I've had a friend who couldn't support my career and made me feel lesser for choosing my path. In those moments, I realized it was okay to let go when the connection no longer served both of us.

It's important to have friends who respect and care for you the same way you care for them. Your mom might be right—sometimes we're better off without people who no longer want to be part of our journey. And while it's hard to see it now, this might be an opportunity for you to find even deeper friendships.

Give yourself time to process your feelings, and trust that new, wonderful friendships are waiting for you ahead.

visualizing myself the way i want to be

From the moment I started dancing, I knew I couldn't live without it. Dance became my voice, my air, my passion—the

only way I could move forward. I had a vision for myself
early on, even before I had the words to fully explain it. I
knew that ABT was the goal. What drew me to ABT wasn't
just its prestige, but also its cultural diversity. While ABT
stood out for embracing a variety of cultures, traditions, and
artistic influences, racially, there was no space for someone
like me at that elite level. Despite the absence of racial diversity, I felt more accepted there than I might have in other
companies. It gave me hope that I could break barriers and
ultimately become the first Black principal ballerina at ABT.

As I grew, so did my dreams. I began to see that my
journey wasn't solely about reaching my own goals—it
was about helping others believe in what's possible. Being
authentic means embracing your real, honest self, even when
it's hard. My responsibility wasn't just to succeed for myself
but to inspire others and show them they belong too. Even
if I didn't become the first Black principal ballerina, simply
being there and sharing my story could make a difference.

Part of that authenticity was embracing my individuality. I wasn't afraid to stand out. My goal was never just
personal success—it was about making ballet accessible to
everyone, not just those who could afford it or traditionally
had access to it. That became one of my driving forces.

Visualization became one of the tools that helped me stay on my path. Visualization is when you create a clear picture in your mind of something you want to achieve, almost like watching a movie of your goals. It became almost like a ritual for me—not only for preparing for performances but for shaping the long-term direction of my life. I would lie in bed at night visualizing the way I wanted a performance to go, the movements I wanted to feel fluid and strong. I could see myself executing each step perfectly, but more importantly, I would see the emotions and the stories I wanted to convey. I also used visualization to imagine my future, the kind of artist I wanted to be, the people I wanted to inspire, and the message I wanted to send through my dancing.

Staying aligned with that vision required a lot of authenticity. I had to know who I was and what I stood for. There were times when I had to go against the grain, against common advice, to stay aligned with my goals. People might have told me to focus on fitting in, to follow a path that had already been carved by others. But I had to trust myself and the vision I saw for my life and career, even when it felt uncertain.

Visualization and authenticity go hand in hand. Visualizing where you want to go helps you stay focused on your goals, and staying authentic keeps you grounded in who you are. I knew that the path I imagined for myself was unique to me, and that's what made it powerful. When you can see yourself clearly—both in where you want to go and in who you truly are—you have everything you need to make your vision come to life.

So, if it's about dancing, art, or any other dream, visualize the path you want to take. But more than that, stay true to who you are as you walk that path. Sometimes, it will mean going against what others expect, but the most important thing is to trust yourself and the vision you've created.

"Dear Misty, I've watched you dance, and you seem so confident all the time. Are you always confident? what do you do if you ever feel like you aren't good enough?"

I want to be honest; confidence isn't something that comes easily all the time. In fact, it's something I have to work at every day, and it's a struggle that everyone experiences, no matter how successful they seem. Confidence doesn't just appear—it's something you build through effort, experience, and self-belief.

I believe confidence comes from a place of love, grounding, community, and support. By grounding, I mean staying connected to what's real and true for me—my values, my passions, and the things that make me feel strong and steady, no matter what's happening around me. These have been the most important elements for me, more than simply trying to "be confident." Surrounding myself with people who lift me up and remind me of my worth has been crucial in moments of doubt.

There have been times when I've struggled with self-doubt or made mistakes, both on and off the stage. But I've come to realize that it's not about being perfect. What really counts is the essence of who I am in those performances, not the mistakes. It's also about who I am as a person—how I show up in the world, in my community, and with my friends and family.

If you ever feel like you're not good enough, know that it's normal to feel that way sometimes—it's part of being human. Confidence is not something you achieve once and keep forever. It's something you build and nurture over time by staying grounded in who you are and surrounding yourself with love and support. Keep working at it and remember that what truly defines you is who you are on the inside.

"Dear Misty, all my friends have long, straight, or wavy hair, and they all wear makeup. My hair is super curly, and I wear it in one big Afro puff most of the time. I don't like makeup. I like to be natural. They want to give me a makeover, but I don't want them to. It's not permanent, though. Should I just let them?"

I love that you're embracing your natural hair and style! Being comfortable in your own skin is so powerful, and it sounds like you already have a strong sense of what makes you feel confident.

I understand how hard it can be when your friends want you to change, even if it's just for fun. But how do *you* feel? If you don't want a makeover, you absolutely don't have to do it. You should never feel pressured to change something about yourself that you love, just to fit in.

It took time for me to stand up for who I am and address these same kinds of issues. I had to fight to wear makeup that was the right shade for my skin when I was onstage. There were moments when I had to tell people that my hair and makeup wouldn't look like the person's next to me—because I'm not them. It wasn't easy, and it took time, but gradually I built the confidence to say, "This is who I am, and I love it." Fighting for these things, though they might have seemed small to others, became a big part of why I have the inner self-confidence I have today.

Your curly hair and natural style are part of what makes you unique, and that's something to celebrate. You get to decide how you want to present yourself to the world, and your friends should respect that. Maybe you can talk to them about how you feel—true friends will understand and support you no matter what.

At the end of the day, what's most important is that you feel comfortable and confident in your own skin. You are beautiful just the way you are, and it's okay to say no if something doesn't feel right to you—even if it's temporary.

setting goals and staying the course

Having a goal has always been how my family and I kept going. Back then, our goal was simple: to survive each day. But that experience taught me something important about setting goals and sticking to them. It set the tone for how I would approach goals throughout my life. The first goal I set for myself, separate from my family, was when I decided I wanted to join the drill team when I was thirteen. I didn't have any dance experience, just a lot of passion and excitement. Even though people told me it might be too hard or that I wasn't ready, I didn't give up. I stuck with it. And what I learned is that it wasn't just about making the team—it was about the journey of trying, growing, and staying focused, even in the face of challenges.

When I think about that time trying to join the drill team, I remember that it wasn't just about the final goal. There were many smaller goals along the way. I had to get my mind and body ready, choreograph a routine, build up the courage to tell my family what I wanted to do, and then practice until I felt confident enough to audition. Every single step helped me grow. Even if I hadn't made the team, the process would have been worth it because I learned so much along the way.

This same idea of setting smaller goals has guided me throughout my life. When I set a big goal—like becoming a principal dancer with American Ballet Theatre—I knew it wouldn't happen overnight. There were so many smaller goals along the way: improving my dance technique, performing well in each role, building my stamina, and learning how to handle the pressure of it all. Each of those steps brought me closer to my big goal, but more importantly, they helped me become the person I needed to be to achieve it.

What I've realized is that sticking to your goals, even when things get tough, is what leads to real success. Setting goals gave me stability when things felt uncertain and helped me find consistency in my life. It's not just about reaching the goal but about the journey of pushing yourself, learning, and growing. Each step you take matters, and when you finally reach your goal, those steps make the achievement even more meaningful.

No matter what your goal is, remember that the process is just as important as the outcome. The small steps, the challenges, and the lessons you learn along the way are what make achieving your goals so special.

"Dear Misty, have you ever set a goal, like winning a competition or getting a role in a show, but didn't succeed? How did you deal with it?"

Yes, I've definitely set goals that I didn't achieve right away, and one experience really stands out. At ABT, we don't usually compete for roles in the way you might imagine a sports tryout, but it does happen occasionally. One year, we were preparing to perform a famous ballet called *La Bayadère*. It's a beautiful ballet full of dramatic storytelling and challenging dancing. The lead character, Gamzatti, is known for being a powerful and technically demanding role.

I was one of two dancers chosen to learn Gamzatti, which was exciting but also nerve-racking. Usually, casting decisions are made based on the artistic director's vision, but this time, the other dancer and I had to audition directly for it. That meant we were being compared in every way— our dancing, our acting, and even how we connected with the character. It felt intense, and I put so much pressure on myself to be perfect.

When the decision came, I wasn't chosen. The artistic staff explained that there weren't enough performances that season to give both of us a chance, so I'd have to wait until the following year. At first, I felt so disappointed. I had worked hard and really wanted the role, so it was difficult not to feel like I'd failed.

But what's important is that setbacks like this don't mean you've failed—they just give you more time to grow. Instead of focusing on what I didn't get, I decided to focus on what I could control. I worked hard on my technique, studied the role more deeply, and found ways to express Gamzatti's emotions even better. When the opportunity came the next season, I felt even more prepared and confident.

Looking back, I see that the journey of working toward the role, despite not going as planned, was just as important as the moment I finally performed it. Not getting the role right away gave me the chance to learn more about myself, grow as a dancer, and understand that success is about more than just the final outcome.

That's why, if you ever feel like you didn't succeed, remember that it's not the end of your story. Sometimes, the hardest moments are the ones that teach you the most. Keep going, keep learning, and know that every step you take is helping you become the person you're meant to be.

"Dear Misty, what if I change my mind about a goal, like wanting to quit a sport or switch hobbies? Does that mean I failed?"

Changing your mind about a goal doesn't mean you've done anything wrong—it's actually a brave and important part of growing and discovering who you are. Sometimes, what feels right for us at one point in our lives changes as we grow, and that's okay. Success isn't about sticking to a goal just because you started it; it's about what makes you happy.

I've had moments where I faced something similar.

Once, I was on tour and scheduled to perform the lead role in *Giselle*, one of the most iconic ballets in the world. It's a role I had dreamed of dancing for years, and I had worked so hard to prepare. But just before the performance, I started experiencing severe back pain. After seeing a physical therapist, I learned I had a stress fracture and would have to pull out of the show. People had traveled from far away to see me, and I worried they'd be disappointed or think I was quitting.

But deep down, I knew that pushing through the pain would only hurt me more and might even keep me from dancing for a long time. My goal had to change—it was no longer about that one performance. It became about healing so I could continue dancing for years to come.

What I learned from that experience is that changing your mind or adjusting your goals isn't giving up—it's honoring what's best for you in the moment. It takes courage to listen to your heart and trust what feels right, even if it means taking a different path than you originally planned.

So if you feel like switching hobbies or quitting a sport is what's best for you, that's completely okay. It's important that you're making a choice that aligns with who you are and what makes you happy. You get to define your journey, and when you make decisions that feel authentic to you, you're showing strength, not failure.

Remember, it's not about sticking to the original plan no matter what—it's about staying connected to what inspires you and helps you grow. That's what real success looks like.

Feeling at Home in Your Own Body

We only get one body, and it's our job to treat it with love and respect. A healthy body image isn't just about how you look—it's about how you feel in your own skin, how you take care of yourself, and how you appreciate what your body can do. Feeling at home in your own body means learning to love and respect it for its strength, uniqueness, and beauty.

When I was younger, I didn't always feel that way. I didn't grow up with access to healthy food or an understanding of what it meant to be healthy. Exercise wasn't a regular part of my life, and when I started dancing, I struggled to fit in. I didn't look like the other dancers—I had a more athletic build and curves, while many of them were thinner and taller. I remember being told as a young ballerina that I needed to lose weight, which was really tough to hear. It made me question if I belonged in ballet at all and left me feeling like I had to change who I was to fit. Food became my way of dealing with stress, but instead of helping, it just made me feel worse. Over time, I realized that being healthy wasn't about trying to look like someone else or meet other people's expectations. It was about figuring out what my body needed and taking care of it in a way that made me feel strong, happy, and ready to do what I love.

When you're dancing, running, creating art, or simply living, your body is there for you. And when you take care of it by eating well, staying active, and surrounding yourself with positive people, you'll start to feel more connected to yourself and more confident.

It's easy to get caught up in what social media or others say about how we should look, but the truth is, there's no one way to be beautiful or healthy. What matters most is how you feel. If you ever feel unsure or uncomfortable in your body, remind yourself that your body is unique, strong, and deserving of love.

As you grow, your body will change, and that's completely normal. What's most important is how you view yourself. Confidence comes from accepting yourself and being kind to your body—every single day.

Wherever you are on your journey, remember: You are

strong, beautiful, and worthy of love and respect. Treat your body like the incredible home it is. Love it, care for it, and let it carry you through all the amazing things you're going to do.

"Dear Misty, I'm smaller than a lot of the other guys in my class, and I feel awkward about how my body looks right now. How do I deal with feeling uncomfortable during these changes?"

It's easy to get caught up in what social media or others say about how we should look, but the truth is, there's no one way to be beautiful or healthy. What matters most is how you feel. If you ever feel unsure or uncomfortable in your body, remind yourself that your body tells your story, one that is worthy of care, respect, and love. When I was growing up, I went through puberty much later than most people—at nineteen—while I was already performing professionally. It was scary to experience something so personal in such a public way. I felt out of place and unsure of how to navigate it, especially when I compared myself to others who seemed to have it all together.

What I learned is that these feelings are normal, and

there are no shortcuts when it comes to growing into your body. It takes time, and yes, it can feel awkward and overwhelming. What helped me most was finding people I trusted—those who didn't judge me and who supported me through the process. They reminded me that it's okay to feel out of place sometimes because it's all part of growing up.

Your body is going through normal changes, even if they don't feel normal right now. You might feel uncomfortable or even left behind, but this is temporary. Surround yourself with people who make you feel good about who you are. Take care of your body by staying active, eating well, and getting enough rest—those small things can make a big difference. Most importantly, be patient with yourself. Your body is growing at its own pace.

Remember, you are amazing just as you are, even if you feel awkward. These changes are part of your story, and one day, you'll look back and realize they helped you become the strong, confident person you're meant to be.

"Dear Misty, I'd really like to have a healthier body so I'll look better and be healthy. Do you have any tips?"

I love that you're thinking about wanting a healthier body—being healthy is such an important goal! But I also want to remind you that being healthy doesn't mean you have to look a certain way. That fine line between "healthy" and "thin" is something I've struggled with throughout my career as a dancer. What I've discovered is that being healthy is different for everyone. It's not about meeting someone else's idea of what you should look like—it's about doing what makes you feel your best.

For me, I learned that eating foods that were more nutritious, with fewer additives and less sugar, made a big difference in how I felt. I also realized that I was often dehydrated when I thought I was hungry, so I started drinking more water throughout the day. It was surprising how much staying hydrated helped me feel more energized and focused.

When it comes to exercise, I discovered that balance is key. As a dancer, I used to think I had to push myself hard all the time, but I learned that rest is just as important as exercise—if not more. Your body needs time to recover so it can grow stronger and perform its best. Eating right, exercising, and getting enough rest all work together to keep you healthy. I found that I felt so much better when I allowed myself to sleep enough at night or take a short nap during the day if I needed it. Rest isn't a sign of weakness—it's a critical part of staying strong and energized.

Moving your body in ways that feel fun—like dancing, playing outside, or trying a new sport—can also make being active more enjoyable and less like work. It's about finding what feels good for you and your body.

Listen to your body, treat it with kindness, and find the balance that works for you. You're already amazing, and taking care of yourself will only help you feel even better inside and out.

Talking Things Out: The Power of communication and self-Advocacy

Throughout my life, I've had to speak up for myself many times. One thing I've learned is that saying something once isn't always enough. Sometimes you have to keep advocating for yourself, even when it feels like you're repeating yourself. But it's so important to say what you need and deserve, and to do it in the moment.

One time that stands out is when I was still in the corps de ballet at American Ballet Theatre. I wanted to perform more classical ballet roles, like featured soloist parts in ballets such as *Swan Lake* and *Giselle*. These weren't lead roles, but parts like the Peasant Pas de Deux in *Giselle* or the Pas de Trois in *Swan Lake*—challenging and beautiful dances that require a lot of skill and stage presence. I knew I had to talk to Kevin McKenzie, the artistic director, about it. I was really nervous, but I practiced what I wanted to say beforehand so I could be clear about my goals. I made sure I was ready to explain why I felt I was prepared for these opportunities and how I'd worked to be ready for the challenge.

To my surprise, the conversation went well. Kevin listened to me and gave me the chance to perform more classical roles. But that wasn't the end of it. I realized that advocating for yourself isn't something you do just once—it's something you have to keep doing throughout your life. I had to keep reminding people that I wasn't just another versatile dancer who could do modern and contemporary ballet. I was trained in classical ballet, and I wanted to be seen for that.

Advocating for yourself isn't just about asking for things. It's about being open to learning and asking questions too. I didn't just say what I wanted—I asked how I could get better, how I could meet the standards for the roles I wanted. When you approach conversations with respect and a genuine desire to improve, people are more likely to listen and help guide you.

The most important thing to remember is that standing up for yourself is a continuous process. You have to be clear about what you want and be willing to ask for feedback. And sometimes, you'll have to speak up more than once. But when you do it with persistence, kindness, and a willingness to grow, people will take notice, and opportunities will come your way.

If there's something you want—such as a new opportunity, a role, or even just recognition—don't be afraid to speak up. And if you have to do it more than once, that's okay. Keep pushing forward and advocating for yourself with confidence and a kind heart. You never know what doors will open when you do!

"Dear Misty, I just got a c-minus on a project, even though I worked really hard. I feel like I wasn't judged fairly and want to talk to my teacher about it. Do you have any examples of when you had to stand up for yourself? How did you do it?"

I completely understand how frustrating it is when you've worked really hard on something and don't feel like your effort was reflected in the result. I've been in similar situations many times, where I didn't get what I felt I deserved. It's hard, but it can also be a really valuable learning experience.

One thing that's helped me a lot in these moments is having someone I trust to talk things out with. I've found that practice conversations with a friend or someone close can be really valuable. They can act as a sounding board, listen to how I'm feeling, and give me some perspective on the situation. Once I've talked it through with someone else, I have a clearer idea of how to approach the conversation and what I want to say.

It's also important to remember that speaking up can give you more insight. Even though it's not always easy, talking to your teacher and asking for feedback can help you understand why you were given the grade you received. Knowledge is power, and getting tips and advice on how you can improve will make you even stronger the next time around. So when you talk to your teacher, explain how hard you worked, but also be open to learning about what could be done differently next time. That way, it becomes not just about the grade but about your growth and development.

Speaking up for yourself is important, and every time you do it, you get more confident in those situations. I'm proud of you for wanting to take that step—you've got this!

"Dear Misty, My best friend, Taylor, has been spending a lot of time with a new group of friends, and I've been feeling left out. I know I need to tell Taylor how I feel, but I hate confrontation and don't want to start an argument. How do I bring it up without causing a fight?"

It's so tough to bring up feelings like this, especially when you care so much about your friendship. It's hard not to feel hurt when you're being left out, but at the same time, you don't want to cause tension between you and Taylor. The good news is that it's possible to have a conversation like this without starting a fight—it's all about how you approach it.

One of the best things you can do is focus on *how* you say it. Instead of accusing or blaming, talk about how *you* feel. You might say something like, "I've been feeling a little left out lately, and I miss hanging out with you." By framing it as your experience and how you're feeling, it's less likely to come across as an attack and more as an honest conversation. Remember, Taylor might not even realize that their actions have hurt you, so giving them a chance to understand your side could actually bring you closer.

It can also help to approach the conversation calmly,

when you're both in a good space to talk. Maybe it's over a walk or a quiet moment, rather than in the heat of the moment when emotions are high. Having a calm, respectful conversation where you express your feelings shows that you care about the friendship and want to make things better, not create more tension.

You're allowed to share your feelings, and you can do it in a way that opens up understanding rather than conflict. Talking about it takes courage, and that matters.

mentorship: Guiding and Being Guided

Mentors have played such an important role in my life and career. I've been really lucky to have many mentors through-out my journey. Some were with me for a long time, and others for just a short while. But each of them made a dif-ference, and that's the beautiful thing about mentorship—it can shape your path in ways you might not expect.

One of my most important mentors was Raven Wilkinson. Raven was the first Black ballerina to perform with Ballet Russe de Monte Carlo, an amazing achievement at a time when ballet was not open to dancers of color. Sadly, she faced so much racism that she was eventually forced to leave the company. Raven's strength and perseverance really inspired me. When I was a young adult in New York City, I wanted to learn more about the history I'm a part of as a Black ballerina and came across Raven's incredible story. I was stunned to discover that she lived just a block away from me! I gathered the courage to reach out to her, and we eventually met. That first meeting felt like stepping into history—Raven's warmth and wisdom drew me in immediately. We connected deeply, sharing stories and experiences, and from that day, a beautiful mentorship and friendship began.

Her story gave me hope and made me realize that I wanted to continue the journey she had started, even though she didn't have the chance to finish it. Raven showed me the power of resilience and how important it is to honor those who came before us while carving our own paths forward.

The impact Raven had on me reminds me of how powerful mentorship can be. When someone who's walked the path before you believes in you, it can change everything. That's why I've found so much joy in becoming a mentor myself.

I often meet young dancers—through letters, messages on social media, backstage after performances, or through the Misty Copeland Foundation. When I'm guiding dancers at ABT, helping young professionals in other companies, or working with students from diverse backgrounds, mentorship is about more than advice. It's about showing them they belong, that their voice matters, and that they can achieve amazing things.

Mentorship is not just about learning new skills; it's about building relationships that offer encouragement and support. When you're being mentored or you're the one mentoring someone else, those connections can open doors, create opportunities, and inspire you to keep growing. It's a reminder that we're never alone on our journey—there's always someone who can guide us or someone we can help along the way.

"Dear Misty, I saw a video of you talking about how a dancer that came before you mentored you and helped you become a ballerina too. I want to be an artist who illustrates books, but I don't know anyone who does that. They're all famous people I'll probably never meet. How can I find a mentor?"

Not all mentors are people we meet in person, and sometimes, the people who inspire us the most may seem out of reach. But here's something I've learned: Mentors don't always have to be famous or well-known. They can be people in your community, at your school, or even online. Sometimes, the best mentors are those who are only a little further along the path than you—those who aren't experts yet but have more experience and can share what they've learned.

If you're looking for someone in the art world, try reaching out to local art teachers, artists, or even librarians who may know of illustrators or art groups in your area. You can also participate in online workshops, classes, or forums where artists share their work and experiences. Many professional illustrators are part of online courses or host Q&A sessions where aspiring artists can learn from them. Even though you might not meet them in person, these safe, organized spaces can still provide valuable advice and guidance.

Another thing to remember is that mentorship can come from unexpected places. Some of my most valuable mentors weren't dancers, but they helped shape me as a person and artist in ways I never expected.

For example, one of my mentors is a television writer and producer who taught me the importance of professionalism and telling my story authentically. Another is an actress who encouraged me to embrace my individuality, and one is a model who shared lessons about confidence and speaking up for myself.

You might find that someone who's not an illustrator, but who is creative and passionate about art, can be just as helpful in guiding you on your journey.

Don't be afraid to reach out to people you admire, even if it feels a little scary at first. You never know who might be willing to help or offer advice. Keep pursuing your passion and remember that mentorship comes in many forms. I'm cheering you on as you work toward becoming the amazing illustrator you're meant to be!

> "Dear Misty, a lady in my neighborhood trains service dogs. I would love to learn how to do that too. I want her to teach me how, but I'm a little afraid to ask. How can I show her that I'd be a good student so she'd be interested in helping me?"

I understand how it can be a little scary to ask someone for help, especially when it's for something you're really passionate about. But you're already showing that you'd be a great student just by thinking about how to approach her.

I've often sought guidance from people who seemed too busy, but by approaching them with confidence, a clear request, and respect, I was usually met with warmth and helpful advice. When you show clarity in your intentions and follow up consistently, people take you seriously, and that's how meaningful relationships can begin.

You can start by expressing your admiration for the work she does and telling her how eager you are to learn. People love to hear that their work is inspiring others, and your enthusiasm will go a long way. You can also offer to help out with anything, even small tasks, to show you're serious about learning and willing to put in the effort.

I know it can be a little intimidating, but if you approach her with kindness and confidence, I'm sure she'll see how much you care. Even if she can't take you on as a student right away, showing that you're willing to put in the time and learn can open the door to other opportunities.

THIRD POSITION

"Relevé"—rise above challenges

IN BALLET, A *RELEVÉ (REH—LUH—VAY)* IS THE graceful rise of the body onto the balls of the feet, either with a smooth lift or a slight spring. It represents strength, balance, and control.

In life, too, we must rise to face challenges, lifting ourselves up with resilience and grace. Each time you choose to rise above what holds you back, you grow stronger. How you approach life's obstacles—with steady focus or an energetic leap—is less important than having the courage to rise. As in ballet, your grace in overcoming challenges becomes a defining part of who you are.

Dear Reader,

In ballet, a relevé *is a move that reminds you to believe in yourself, even if you wobble along the way. Life can feel like that too: Sometimes you fall; sometimes things don't go as planned. But each time you rise, you're a little stronger, a little wiser, and even a bit more resilient.*

For me, rising above challenges has meant learning from my mistakes and turning setbacks into growth. Believe it or not, some of my best lessons have come from falling or even facing injury. Those moments weren't easy, but they taught me things I couldn't learn any other way. I've learned to laugh at myself and find the humor in moments that might seem daunting because, let's face it, everyone stumbles at some point. Mistakes might feel tough, but they're also what make life interesting and give us stories to tell.

Remember, mistakes aren't failures; they're stepping stones to growth. So when things don't go perfectly, don't be afraid to laugh a little, dust yourself off, and try again. Rising above challenges isn't about being perfect; it's about embracing the journey, believing in yourself, and learning from each step, even the wobbly ones.

Here are a few things that have helped me along the way:

imposter syndrome

Have you ever felt like you don't belong or that everyone around you is more talented, smarter, or just better at something? That feeling has a name—it's called imposter syndrome. It's when self-doubt creeps in, making you feel like you're not good enough or that you don't deserve your achievements, despite working hard to get there. Imposter syndrome isn't an obstacle you can see or touch; it's a challenge that forms in your own mind, fueled by doubts and insecurities. But that doesn't make it any less real or tough to face.

I've faced imposter syndrome at different stages in my life and career. When I joined the drill team as captain in middle school even though I had no dance training, I felt like an outsider. I questioned if I was capable and if I even deserved to lead.

Later, as I entered the ballet world at thirteen, those feelings showed up in new ways. Starting dance late and looking different from other dancers—being Black, athletic, and curvy—brought its own set of judgments and even discrimination. I began to question if I truly belonged in a world where I stood out so much.

As my career grew and I explored roles beyond ballet—writing books, producing films, designing fashion—those feelings resurfaced. I'd wonder, "Am I really qualified for this?" But I began to realize that my life experiences and unique perspective were what made my contributions valuable. My journey allowed me to express different parts of myself and connect with others in a meaningful way.

The tricky thing about imposter syndrome is that it can feel very real and convincing. An imposter is someone who is pretending to be something—or someone—they aren't. When you feel like an imposter, those doubts and insecurities may seem true, but they don't define who you are or what you're capable of. Over time, I learned to recognize these thoughts as just that—thoughts. They don't hold the power to decide my worth unless I let them. Each time I remind myself that I've earned my place through hard work, that I belong, and that I am capable, those doubts lose a little bit of their strength.

It's also helpful to know that imposter syndrome is something almost everyone faces at some point, even those who seem the most confident. If those "imposter" thoughts creep in, remember that you are exactly where you're meant to be. Every small act of confidence is like taking a step forward, building resilience against self-doubt.

In this section, you'll find tips and stories that can help you face imposter syndrome. Remember, self-doubt is not uncommon on the path to discovering your true strength. You are more than enough, and you deserve to be right where you are.

"Dear Misty, my teacher told me the story I wrote is really good, and she wants me to read it in front of the class. I don't think it's that good and I'm worried people will either laugh at me or tell me I think I'm better than them. should I just tell her I don't want to?"

First, let me say how incredible it is that your teacher loved your story so much that she wants the whole class to hear it! That's a huge compliment and shows just how special your work is. It's normal to feel nervous about sharing something personal, especially when it's creative. I totally understand—you can feel vulnerable, and it's easy to worry about how others will react.

But here's the thing: If you wrote something from your heart, then it's worth sharing. When I started writing, I had doubts too. I wondered if people would judge me or think I was trying to prove something. But I realized that my words could inspire others, and encouragement from mentors, family, and friends gave me the strength to focus on what I loved.

If you're proud of your story, take a deep breath, stand tall, and trust yourself. Sharing it doesn't mean you're saying you're better than anyone else—it just means you're being brave enough to let others see a little piece of who you are. And who knows? Your story might just inspire someone else to share their voice too.

So go ahead and be bold. You're stronger and more capable than you know, and your voice deserves to be heard!

"Dear Misty, this weekend I was at a gymnastics meet, and I was excited until I saw everyone else warming up. They all looked so strong and graceful, and way better than me. I wanted to go home! My mom made me stay. Do you ever feel like that? What do you do?"

It's so natural to look around, see others who seem so strong and graceful, and start to doubt yourself. Sometimes, we're our own toughest critics, especially when everyone else looks like they have it all together.

Here's a story from my own experience: Even though I'm a ballet dancer, a choreographer I had worked with many times recommended me to audition for a Broadway show she had choreographed and written. This show required not only a strong dance background but also extensive gymnastics training, which I didn't have. When I saw the others warming up, they looked so experienced, and I felt completely out of place. I remember thinking, "Why am I here?"

But then I reminded myself: The choreographer saw something special in me and believed I could bring something unique to her show. I had to trust that. So I focused on what *I* could bring to the audition and gave it my best. It turned out to be an incredible experience—one that taught me so much about believing in myself, even in moments when I felt like an outsider.

Next time you're at a meet, take a deep breath and remember your own strengths. Focus on what *you* can do, not on how others look. Competing is as much about showing up with confidence as it is about any skill or move. Be proud of yourself for being brave enough to put yourself out there and for giving it your all.

Feeling Stuck

Sometimes, the hardest challenges don't come from the outside—they come from within. There are seasons when that spark fades, and you're left feeling stuck or unmotivated, like you're just going through the motions. I've been there too. At one point, I went through almost an entire year feeling uninspired to dance or create. I had reached major milestones, including becoming a principal dancer, but I found myself questioning if what I was doing was truly challenging me or making the impact I wanted in the ballet world. After twenty years at ABT, I felt like I needed to be doing more—work that would push boundaries and help ballet become more inclusive and accessible.

During that time, I started thinking about creating the Misty Copeland Foundation. The idea of using my experiences to support young dancers and make ballet more inclusive reignited my motivation. It gave me a sense of purpose and reminded me why I fell in love with dance in the first place.

I also realized that instead of forcing myself to feel motivated, I needed to take a different approach. I began experimenting, giving myself the freedom to rediscover ballet with fresh eyes. I tried new routines, approached my cross-training with curiosity, and found ways to mix up my practice. I allowed myself to explore, and by doing so, I opened doors to learning in ways I hadn't before.

Boredom and feeling stuck are normal, but they can also be opportunities. I've learned that it's okay to feel this way—it's often a sign that you need a change in routine or a fresh outlook. One of the biggest lessons I took away was the importance of staying open to new experiences. Switching things up, trying something new, or even taking a break can help you reconnect with what you love most.

Sometimes, all it takes is giving yourself the space to try something different and adjust your routine. Allowing yourself to experiment, without the pressure to be perfect, can help reignite that spark when you least expect it.

"Dear Misty, it's winter break, and I've been looking forward to working on a sculpture for my art class. Now I don't want to do it. I look at the lump of clay and then I go watch TV instead. I don't understand why I can't even start on something I was excited about."

It's totally normal to feel stuck, even if it's something you were excited about. I've felt that way too—whether it's with ballet, writing, or any creative project. Sometimes, just looking at a blank page or an empty studio can feel overwhelming, and the initial excitement fades.

Here's something that helps me in moments like these: Start small. Take just one tiny step. Pick up the clay, make one shape, or try a simple movement. Often, just going through the motions—even if it feels like nothing special at first—can spark ideas and motivation. You don't have to finish it all at once; just take it one small step at a time.

And remember, it's okay if today isn't the day you feel inspired. Every day is another chance to try again, and some days will feel more creative than others. Trust that your ideas and energy will come back in their own time. When they do, you'll be glad you took those first steps, even if they felt small.

"Dear Misty, our school is having a read-athon, and the prize is a $100 gift card for the bookstore. I was in the lead for two weeks, and now it's taking me forever to finish the book I'm on. somebody just passed me. How can I speed up again?

Leading the read-athon for two weeks is an amazing accomplishment! It's natural to feel pressured to pick up speed again, especially when there's a prize at stake. It's something I've dealt with too—during long performance seasons, I sometimes want to spend every spare moment rehearsing, even on my day off. But I've learned that pushing too hard can actually slow me down, leaving me tired and less focused.

Sometimes, the best thing you can do is give yourself a little breather. I know it can be hard to relax when there's still a big goal ahead, but stepping away for a moment can truly help. Try reading somewhere different, like outside in the fresh air, or with a family member or close friend. Changing the setting or sharing the experience with someone can make it more enjoyable.

When you come back to your book, you might find you have more energy and focus to enjoy it again. And remember, you're already doing an amazing job! Reading isn't just about speed—it's about connecting with the story and letting it inspire you. Set a steady pace, and trust that every page you turn brings you closer to your goal.

Handling Disappointment or Defeat

Disappointment is something we all experience, no matter how much we prepare or how hard we work. It could be about missing out on something you were looking forward to or not achieving the outcome you hoped for. When things don't go as planned, it's normal to feel sad or frustrated. But remember, even though it hurts, it doesn't mean your journey is over. Sometimes, setbacks open up new paths we hadn't considered.

I know this from personal experience. One of my biggest disappointments was having to change ballet studios at fifteen. I had been living with my ballet teacher since I was thirteen, catching up on training and becoming part of her family. I saw her as my guide and imagined my future with her helping me reach my dreams. But then my mom decided it was time for me to move back home to focus on family, which was heartbreaking for all of us. Leaving the only ballet teacher I'd known felt like my world was falling apart, and I had to start over in a new environment.

Over time, though, I found that ballet itself became my anchor. Even though my dance teacher, dance studio, and second family were gone, dance wasn't. My passion for dance gave me strength, despite losing the stability I thought I needed. Slowly, I adjusted, and I learned that even if the path looks different from what we planned, we can still find our way.

If you're facing disappointment, it's okay to feel those emotions, but also remember that it's not the end. Take it one step at a time, focus on what you love, and trust that you'll find your way. You may even discover a strength you didn't know you had, just like I did.

> *"Dear Misty, my basketball team lost the championship game by one point at the buzzer. At the team party I cried. I wanted to win so badly. I'm still depressed, and it was a week ago. How do you deal with that kind of disappointment?"*

It's completely normal to feel disappointed—even a week later. When we care deeply about something, those feelings don't just go away overnight. It's okay to let yourself feel sad; it shows how much this mattered to you.

I remember a similar experience from when I was twenty-five. I was chosen by my artistic director to compete in a prestigious ballet competition called the Erik Bruhn Prize. Participating in this competition is one of the highest honors in ballet, with the opportunity for a cash prize, a medal, and the immense prestige of winning. Dancers from top companies around the world were invited, and just being selected felt like a huge achievement. I prepared by rehearsing for months—on top of the eight-hour rehearsal days I was already doing. I poured everything I had into it and felt incredible about what I put onstage.

But I lost.

I felt all the emotions you're describing. But something unexpected happened afterward. The dancer who won was incredibly talented, and like me, she was a brown girl in a field where there were few of us. We connected over our shared experiences, and she became a good friend. That sense of support and connection was incredibly meaningful.

What I learned from that experience was that there's so much more to gain than just winning. I may not have taken home the prize, but I showed up, gave my best, and grew from it. A few months later, I was promoted to soloist, and I believe it was because of how I handled myself through that loss.

With that in mind, if you're feeling down, give yourself time to process it. And when you're ready, think about what this experience can teach you. Each game, win or lose, shapes who you are as a player and as a person. Remember, every great player has faced setbacks—it's what you do after the loss that really counts.

Keep playing, keep learning, and remember that this is just one step in your journey.

"Dear Misty, I was so close to winning the spelling bee, but I messed up on a word in the last round. I keep replaying it in my head and feel like I failed. How do you deal with messing up in front of people?"

It's normal to replay it in your mind and feel like that one moment defines everything. But here's something I've learned: Most people remember how you made them feel, not the little mistakes you made. Your effort, heart, and courage shine much brighter than any slip-up.

I've had my share of stumbles too. I've fallen onstage, forgotten choreography, and even made mistakes in front of a whole classroom.

One time, when I was on tour in Tokyo, Japan, I was performing a featured soloist role called the Flower Girl in the ballet *Don Quixote* on opening night. During my solo variation, I approached the first big jump—and fell flat on my face. I could hear the audience gasp so loudly it drowned out the orchestra.

But I got up with pride and told myself I had nothing to

lose. I jumped as high as I could and finished the variation strong, with confidence. By the end, the audience went wild. That moment taught me that even when things go wrong, how you respond matters more than the mistake itself.

Be kind to yourself and focus on what you accomplished. You made it to the last round—that's amazing! Think of how much effort and focus it took to get there. And you did it by being yourself, which is the most powerful thing of all.

Messing up isn't the end of the story—it's just one chapter. Keep being brave, keep learning, and remember that every experience, even the tough ones, helps you grow.

when Life Happens

Sometimes, life's stress can feel so big that it even shows up in our bodies. Maybe you've felt it—a stomachache before school, a headache that won't go away, or just feeling so tired that you want to hide from everything. When life feels overwhelming, our bodies often react in surprising ways.

When I was younger, I struggled with terrible migraines. These headaches would get so intense that I'd have to leave school early or spend hours lying in a dark room. I didn't realize it back then, but a lot of those migraines were caused by emotional stress. Between the ages of two and thirteen, there was only one short period where we had a stable home. Most of the time, we struggled to have enough food, and that constant uncertainty created a tense and unpredictable environment.

As a kid, I didn't know how to process those big feelings or how much they were affecting me. Up until I was seventeen, those migraines were a regular part of my life.

Things started to change when ballet entered my world. Ballet gave me something steady to hold on to and a way to release my emotions. When I eventually moved away to dance professionally, the migraines began to ease. I was finding healthy ways to manage my stress, and ballet became an outlet to express myself.

If you're dealing with stress—from friendships, family, school, or anything else—realize that your body may be trying to tell you it needs care and attention, not just your mind. It's normal to feel overwhelmed sometimes, and it's important to acknowledge those feelings rather than push them away. Talking to someone you trust, like a friend, teacher, or family member, can make a huge difference. Just saying what's on your mind can lighten the load. Taking little breaks for yourself and doing something that calms you can give your mind a much-needed rest.

And don't forget to care for your body, too; simple

things like going for a walk, getting fresh air, or taking deep breaths can ease some of the tension you're feeling.

Stress is something everyone deals with, and learning to handle it takes time. You're not alone, and with a little patience and some healthy ways to cope, things can get easier. Whatever you're going through, it's all part of growing up—and you're doing an amazing job.

> "Dear Misty, it seems like everything bad is happening to me. My best friend isn't talking to me. My coach benched me for messing up a play, and now my parents are getting a divorce. I cried in bed last night. You always look so calm and relaxed in your ballet pictures. Do you have any advice?"

Have you ever heard the expression "when it rains, it pours"? When it feels like everything is going wrong all at once, it's completely natural to feel overwhelmed and alone. Life can be really tough, and sometimes it seems like everything is piling up, making it hard to see a way through.

I've had times like that too. I remember a period when I was dealing with the worst injury of my career and going through a painful breakup at the same time. It felt like no matter what I did, I couldn't shake that heavy feeling. What helped me through was finding balance in the things that grounded me, like dance, and leaning on the people who cared about me—my mentors, friends, and family.

If you're feeling overwhelmed, try finding small ways to bring yourself comfort, like working on a hobby, or even cuddling up with a favorite book. It doesn't have to be anything big; sometimes a small distraction can give your heart and mind a break. Remember, you don't have to carry all this alone. Reaching out to people who care about you can be incredibly comforting.

Life can feel overwhelming sometimes, but these tough times don't define you. They're just one chapter in your story. Take things one day at a time and remember to be gentle with yourself.

"Dear Misty, lately I'm sad all the time. I can't focus, and I feel nervous for no reason. I don't want to do anything, and I just want to be alone in my room. I don't know what's wrong with me. what should I do?"

Thank you for sharing how you're feeling—it's really brave to reach out, especially when things feel heavy and hard to understand. I want you to know that you're not alone. Many people go through times when they feel sad or anxious, or just want to be alone. It's okay to feel this way, even if you don't know exactly why.

When I was fifteen, I went through a period that felt similar. I had just moved back to live with my mom and siblings in a small motel room after living with my ballet teacher for a few years. Suddenly, everything felt overwhelming, and I didn't feel like I had any hope for the future. I remember spending hours alone, crying and listening to music, trying to make sense of it all. Looking back, I realize that I was going through something very close to what we call depression.

Talking to friends and, later, to new teachers helped me work through those feelings. Sometimes, the healthiest way to handle overwhelming emotions is to share them with people who care about us. Just speaking what's in your heart can be a huge relief and can make you feel a little less alone.

If these feelings continue, it's important to take another step. Consider talking to a school counselor or a teacher you trust, or asking an adult to help you make an appointment with a therapist or doctor. They can help you understand what you're feeling and work with you to find ways to feel better. You don't have to face this alone—there are people who want to support you and help you stay safe and healthy.

Take things one step at a time and remember that brighter days are ahead. Opening up to someone you trust, even if it's just a little each day, can make a big difference. You deserve to feel better, and there's always hope.

changing Bodies and Growing Pains

Growing up is full of changes—some exciting, some confusing, and some downright frustrating. It's normal to feel impatient with your body, especially when it seems like everyone else is changing faster or in different ways. Sometimes, there's pressure to look a certain way or to reach certain milestones that feel "grown-up." I remember feeling that way too.

When I was younger, I was so eager to get my first bra and start shaving my legs. There was a lot of pressure at school to look a certain way, and my two older brothers loved to tease me about being flat-chested and having hairy arms and legs. I remember having full outbursts with my family, insisting that one day I'd have all those "female" attributes I thought I was supposed to have, like fuller breasts and smooth legs. I just wanted to look and feel more like the other girls my age.

But my body had its own timing. I was what people call a "late bloomer" and didn't hit puberty until I was nineteen—right in the middle of my professional ballet career. At the time, I was so focused on dance that these changes felt like they were happening out of nowhere, and I remember thinking, "I waited so long, and now it's happening when I least expect it!"

I've come to understand that our bodies are unique works of art that come into their own when they're ready. It's easy to feel pressured to look a certain way or to rush through these stages, but each of us grows at our own pace, and that's a beautiful thing.

I've also talked to male friends and colleagues about their experiences, and they've shared that they often felt similar pressures. Many of them felt the expectation to look "strong," be tall, or have muscles at a certain age. For some, that same impatience or insecurity lingered because they didn't look like the other boys their age or the images they saw on TV or in magazines. The truth is, these pressures aren't limited to one gender—we all experience them in different ways.

If you're feeling anxious about changes that haven't happened yet—or ones that have—just remember to be patient and gentle with yourself. You're exactly where you're supposed to be, and in time, everything will come together.

Growing up is a journey, and having patience and support along the way can make it a little easier. Trust in your own timing and remember that every stage is part of who you are becoming.

> "Dear Misty, this is kind of embarrassing, but I just started my period. I'm a ballerina, and I'm not sure what to do. I have to wear a leotard and tights. Do you have any advice?"

Don't feel embarrassed—this is such a natural part of life, and every ballerina you look up to has had to figure this out. When I was your age, I felt the same way. My first period didn't come until I was nineteen, and it actually happened onstage during *Swan Lake* at the Metropolitan Opera House. It was a shock because I didn't expect it, and no one had prepared me. But this is part of our journey as women—learning to tune in to our bodies and manage these moments.

One thing I've learned is that everyone's body is different, and there's no "one right way" to handle this. Find what works best for you and remember it's okay to figure it out at your own pace. You might want to keep a small period kit in your dance bag with whatever you need, plus a spare pair of tights, just in case. It can also help to talk through what you're feeling with someone you trust—maybe a friend, a mentor, or another dancer who's been through it. They might even have creative solutions you haven't thought of! Sharing can bring a sense of relief, and you'll find that many people understand and want to support you.

Learning to care for yourself in this way is just as important as any other part of your training.

> *"Dear Misty, my right knee hurts all the time, and I don't even want to play at recess. The doctor said I'll outgrow it, but what am I supposed to do while I wait?"*

First and foremost, make sure you take care of your knee. Your well-being is so important! If it keeps bothering you, I'd suggest talking to your family about getting a second opinion from another doctor. It's always good to have more clarity and options for how to feel your best.

While you're waiting for your knee to heal, this could

be a great time to explore activities that don't require a lot of movement. When I was your age, I spent many recesses and lunch periods quietly with teachers because I was pretty introverted. We'd read, do arts and crafts, or work on creative projects together. Those moments became special—a way to express myself and discover new interests.

Think about what makes you happy or curious—maybe it's drawing, writing stories, building something, or even diving into a fun project like making a scrapbook or researching a topic you love. You'd be surprised at how many exciting things you can explore without needing to run around.

Sometimes, these quiet moments open up a whole new world of possibilities and help you discover things about yourself you didn't know. Take care of yourself, listen to your body, and let your creativity lead the way—I know you'll find something amazing to keep you inspired!

social media: cyberbullying and negative comments

I know how tough it can be to face criticism online. One of the things I love most about performing live is the real-time response from the audience—the energy, the emotions, and the connection. But social media can be very different. While I've made genuine connections on these platforms, it can also feel isolating. Comments often come from people who don't really know you or see you as a real person.

I've had moments where people recorded me after I made a mistake in the theater and shared those clips online with hurtful comments. In the comment sections on social media and YouTube, people would say that I didn't deserve the roles I was dancing or that I wasn't capable of performing them. Some even suggested that I only got opportunities because of my race. Reading those words was hard, and for a long time, I questioned myself because of them.

What helped me was remembering why I do what I do. Ballet is my passion, and I've worked incredibly hard to get where I am. I also remind myself—and my followers—that I'm human. I have feelings, doubts, and strengths, just like everyone else. When I connect with people who support and understand me, it's a powerful reminder that the opinions of strangers don't define me.

The best way to protect yourself on social media is by focusing on what you love. Surround yourself with people who lift you up and remind you of your worth. If the comments ever feel too intense, it's okay to take a break, block negative people, or turn to someone you trust for support. And always remember, you're more than what anyone says about you online.

Reality versus Façade

There's so much pressure to present a "perfect" image on social media, especially as a public figure or a "brand." But I try my best to be me, rather than pretending to be something I'm not. I believe in honoring a healthy body image and being authentic, rather than trying to fit into anyone else's standards. For me, my "brand" has always been about being authentically me.

Sometimes, I'm judged for my unfiltered Blackness—for embracing my natural hair, wearing makeup that works for my skin tone, or speaking up about issues that matter to me, regardless of how it challenges what people expect in ballet. Those things are a core part of who I am, and I'm proud to bring my full, unfiltered self into spaces where it hasn't always been accepted.

When it comes to social media, I focus on sharing things that genuinely matter to me, even if they're not "flawless." My goal is to be real with my followers and show up as myself. Staying true to my values, passions, and beliefs makes my social media presence feel honest and fulfilling. It's about being who I really am, flaws and all, and trusting that the right people will connect with that.

Here's my advice: Remember that social media usually shows only the highlights, not the full story. Imagine someone sharing a picture of an amazing art project they made—it looks incredible, like they just whipped it up in a second. But what you don't see are the moments they struggled to figure out what to draw, the mistakes they erased, or the times they felt frustrated because it didn't look right. In the same way, people post their best moments online, not their struggles, doubts, or mistakes.

Don't feel pressured to compare yourself to the "idealized" things you see online. Being and honoring who you are—your unique personality, culture, and passions—is far more valuable than creating a façade. You deserve to be celebrated for who you truly are, both online and in real life.

Using Social Media for Good

When Instagram first started, I remember feeling this incredible sense of connection—a chance to reach people from all kinds of backgrounds and bring them art. It was everything I'd been working for in my career, following in the footsteps of my idols who wanted to make ballet accessible to as many people as possible. Social media became a bridge, especially for those who don't have a theater in their community, can't afford a ticket to a live show, or simply haven't had the chance to experience ballet.

Using social media for good means sharing what you're passionate about and supporting others. Raising awareness for a cause, sharing something that brings you joy, or lifting up a friend—social media can be a powerful tool for connection and inspiration. Think of it as a way to make a positive impact in your own unique way. Let your voice and your interests shine through, and don't be afraid to show the world what matters to you!

"Dear Misty, social media can be overwhelming sometimes, and I'm not sure who I should follow. How do you decide who to follow?"

I like to follow people and organizations that inspire me, uplift me, or teach me something new. These can be dancers who share their creative journeys, artists and writers who spark my imagination, or organizations doing work

I believe in, like promoting inclusion in the arts or supporting mental health. When I scroll through my feed, I want to feel motivated, not drained. That's why I focus on accounts that align with my values and bring positivity into my life.

Think about what makes you feel happy or inspired. Maybe it's watching a musician practice, learning fun facts about space, or seeing someone bake incredible cakes. Following people who encourage you, celebrate authenticity, and make you feel good about your own journey can really change how you experience social media.

It's also okay to unfollow or mute accounts that don't make you feel good. If you find yourself comparing yourself to others or feeling like certain posts make you doubt your worth, take a step back. Social media should be a tool that supports you, not something that makes you feel bad.

And remember, social media is just one piece of life. Don't be afraid to spend time offline, too! Real-life connections, hobbies, and experiences will always matter more than likes or followers. Surround yourself—online and offline—with people and messages that build you up. Your feed should feel like a space that motivates and supports you, so take control of it and make it work for you!

"Dear Misty, sometimes I look at people's posts online and feel FOMO. Then I feel bad about myself for feeling that way. What can I do?"

First, let's talk about FOMO—it stands for "fear of missing out." It's that feeling you get when you see other people doing something fun or exciting and you wish you were there too. It can make you feel like you're being left out or like everyone else is having a better time than you. Social media can make it seem like everyone else's life is perfect, but the truth is, those posts only show the highlights—not the whole story. Everyone has challenges and struggles, even if they're not visible online.

I've definitely had moments of feeling FOMO. When I was injured and couldn't dance or tour with ABT, it was hard to scroll through posts of my friends performing onstage while I was stuck recovering. Sometimes, it felt like I was missing out on everything, and scrolling only made me feel worse. In those moments, I learned that it's okay to step away and take a break. Giving yourself space can help you focus on your own healing and happiness without the outside pressure of comparing yourself to others.

When those feelings come up, try shifting your focus

to gratitude for your own journey. Think about what's going well in your life or what you're excited to work toward. You can also use others' successes as inspiration rather than competition. Remind yourself that everyone's path is different, and what makes your journey unique is what makes it special.

Most importantly, be kind to yourself! Feeling FOMO doesn't mean you're a bad person—it's just a reminder to reconnect with what matters most to you. Social media is just a small part of life, and it's okay to take breaks and focus on your own goals and happiness.

"Dear Misty, my parents finally let me get on instagram. I follow you! I saw somebody put a really mean comment on one of your posts. what do you do when that happens?"

One of the most important things I've learned on social media is that I don't owe anyone a response, especially when it comes to negativity. I trust my instincts and lean on my support system—the people who know and care about me.

Sometimes, if I feel strong and see a chance for a positive lesson, I might respond to a hurtful comment. But only if I believe it can lead to an important discussion. I've used moments like these to talk about meaningful topics, like race or aspects of performance and technique. I say what I need to, and then I step away, knowing I can't control everyone's opinions.

Remember, it's your space and your journey. Only respond if it feels right and focus on surrounding yourself with people who lift you up. Social media can be a wonderful tool for connection, but your peace always comes first.

"Dear Misty, I'm on TikTok, and I post videos of myself playing piano. Most of the time, people say I'm good. Yesterday this man said I'm pretty and even though it's a compliment, it made me uncomfortable. What should I do?"

It's really important to trust your instincts—when something makes you uncomfortable, it's a signal to pay attention and take action to protect your space. Social media should be a place where you feel safe and respected while sharing what you love, like your amazing piano playing.

You have every right to set boundaries to make sure your experience online feels positive and secure. If a comment doesn't sit right with you, you can block the person who posted it, delete the comment, or report it to the platform. If you're unsure what to do, talk to an adult or someone else you trust who can help you decide the best steps to take.

Sometimes, taking a break from social media can also be helpful. It gives you time to reset, focus on the things you enjoy, and come back when you feel ready. Social media isn't about pleasing everyone—it's about sharing what brings you joy, and you deserve to do that without feeling uneasy or pressured.

Remember, you're in control of your online space. Blocking someone, reporting a comment, or asking for help are all ways to protect yourself—and they're completely okay to do. Stay focused on the joy you feel when you play piano and the positive connections you make online. Your safety and comfort matter most, and you have the power to create an environment that reflects that.

FOURTH POSITION

"Grand Jeté"—Take the Leap

IN BALLET, A *GRAND JETÉ* (*GRAHN ZHUH–TAY*) is a daring leap where one leg is brushed forward and the other is thrown back, creating a moment of flight across the stage.

In life, challenging yourself is like doing a *grand jeté*. It's about pushing yourself to take big leaps, even if you're uncertain of the landing. Each time you dare to reach a little farther or try something new, you build the confidence to tackle bigger challenges. Just like in ballet, the more times you leap, the stronger and more resilient you become.

Dear Reader,
When I think of a grand jeté, *I see more than just*

a graceful movement across the stage—I see a leap of faith, a moment when you push yourself to see how far you can go. Challenging yourself in life is like that grand jeté. *It's about testing your limits and finding the courage to take on something that feels big or a little scary.*

While we all face setbacks and doubts, one of life's greatest rewards is overcoming challenges— especially those we set for ourselves. There's a special satisfaction in reaching a difficult goal, and the journey often matters as much as the goal itself. Goals mean the most when they come from your heart and are driven by passion. Challenging yourself shows you care about growing and learning, whether it's improving at something you love, facing a fear, or trying something new.

There will be times when reaching your goals feels easy and times when it feels like you're leaping into the unknown. It's okay to feel nervous or unsure. What matters is taking that first step and trusting that each leap, no matter how small, helps you grow.

I've learned that the path to challenging your-

self doesn't always go as planned. Sometimes I stumble or take a few wrong steps. But every time I get back up, I remind myself that each challenge is an opportunity to learn, build strength, and discover how high I can soar.

Remember, the most important thing is to keep moving forward, even if it's one small step at a time. With patience and determination, you'll find yourself reaching dreams that once felt out of reach.

Exploring Your Creativity and Talent

When we think of creativity, it's easy to imagine painting, dancing, or writing—but creativity can show up in surprising ways, sometimes in the simplest things we do every day. There are so many forms of talent and intelligence, like the ability to connect with others, solve problems, or understand the natural world. For me, one of my first creative outlets was sewing, something I began when I was just seven years old.

It started with little adjustments to my clothes. I'd shorten straps, take in pants, and add small touches to make my clothes feel like my own. Soon, I was helping my siblings with their clothes and even sewing outfits for my baby dolls. Sewing was something that felt natural to me, a way to work with my hands and bring my ideas to life. I now recognize it as a form of kinesthetic intelligence—an instinctive way of using my hands to create, fix, and shape things.

Later, when I began ballet, this early love for sewing became even more valuable. I learned to sew ribbons and elastics onto my ballet shoes, and when I rented costumes for performances outside of American Ballet Theatre, I would make small alterations to ensure they fit just right. I also would alter my leotards to fit my body, making sure they complemented my movement and gave me confidence. This wasn't just a task; it was a ritual that connected me to my art, a quiet expression of creativity that helped me feel prepared and in control.

Looking back, I see how these small, everyday acts of creativity were clues about who I was becoming. They were little sparks of my creative side, hints of the discipline and attention to detail that ballet would demand of me.

Our talents can sometimes be hidden in our daily activities, waiting for us to recognize them. A gift for understanding people, a talent for making others laugh, or a passion for creating with your hands—each of us has strengths that lead us to be creative in our own unique ways. Sewing was my first love, long before I knew it would help me in my journey as a dancer. So take time to explore the things you enjoy—you may discover talents and passions that are a part of you, waiting to lead you on your own distinct journey.

"Dear Misty, I'm in middle school, and all my friends are involved in interesting things like sports, music, and clubs. I literally have zero talents and can't find anything I want to do. How can I figure out what I'm good at?"

First, let me tell you a secret—not everyone discovers what they're good at right away, and that's completely okay. When I was younger, I didn't start out knowing I would become a dancer. In fact, I didn't even try ballet until I was thirteen! All I knew was that I loved music—it made me feel alive. Because I was open about what I loved, a teacher noticed and encouraged me to try ballet. I wasn't sure it was the right fit at first, but I gave it a shot. That one step opened up a whole new world for me.

Sometimes, figuring out what you're good at starts with curiosity. Think about things that catch your attention or make you wonder, "What if I tried that?" Curiosity is often a sign that you're being pulled in a new direction, even if you're not sure where it will lead.

Maybe you like drawing, cooking, solving puzzles, or spending time with animals. You don't have to be perfect at something to give it a try. Exploring these interests can sometimes uncover hidden talents or passions.

Also, don't overlook the smaller things you're good at—like being a good listener, making people laugh, or encouraging your friends when they need it. Those are real talents too, and they can make a big difference in the world around you. Talents don't always have to look like winning a trophy or being onstage.

Take your time, and don't be afraid to try new things, even if they feel unfamiliar or challenging. Every step you take is a chance to learn something new about yourself. Trust that your journey to discovering your passions and talents is unique and special to you. Sometimes, the things that make you curious today will lead you to something amazing tomorrow.

"Dear Misty, I'm good at a lot of things but don't feel passionate about any of them. How did you find something you really loved?"

It's more common than you might think to be good at different things but not feel deeply connected to any of them.

For me, it was almost the opposite. I didn't feel like I was naturally good at anything right away. Instead, I was searching for something that felt real, something that would bring true meaning to my life.

What I discovered is that passion isn't always about being amazing at something from the start. For me, it began with a feeling—a love for music and art that made me feel alive. I didn't know where that feeling would lead, but I kept following it. Eventually, my love for music turned into a love of movement, and that led me to dance.

Ballet came naturally to me, but what truly made it special was the sense of purpose and joy it brought. It felt worth every moment I spent on it, and that's how I knew it was something I truly cared about.

If you're good at a lot of things but don't feel passionate about any of them, try focusing on what makes you happy or excited.

Is there something you want to keep coming back to, no matter how difficult it gets? Maybe it's something you find yourself inviting friends to join you in, or something you look forward to doing after school. It might even be something you love to watch other people do. These small sparks can be clues to what truly matters to you.

Passion often grows from a deep connection to what you're doing rather than just a skill or talent. So keep exploring, and don't be afraid to let go of things that don't feel meaningful to you. When you find something that feels worth your time and commitment, you'll know it's special. Trust yourself, and give yourself the freedom to follow those sparks wherever they lead.

Trying New Things

Have you ever faced a moment when you had to try something completely new, something that felt way outside your comfort zone? Maybe it was joining a new club, learning a new skill, or trying out for a team. It can be exciting to take on something unfamiliar, but it's also totally normal to feel nervous or unsure. Even as a professional dancer, I've had moments when trying something new felt scary—but those moments often led to amazing growth.

In the last chapter, I told you about my experience being invited to audition for a Broadway show. Since I was a ballet dancer, Broadway wasn't a world I was used to, and it felt very different from the ballet stage. But I was intrigued and decided to go for it. This audition had a big twist, though—I'd be performing alongside gymnasts, and, on top of that,

I'd need to sing! I'd never sung in front of an audience before, and honestly, I had no idea if I'd be any good at it.

When the casting team asked me to sing something on the spot, my mind immediately went to Mariah Carey. I'm a huge fan and know her songs by heart. Mariah is known for her incredible voice and really high notes that only the best singers can reach. When I suggested singing one of her songs, the pianist looked at me with raised eyebrows and asked, "Do you really think you can sing Mariah?" My cheeks turned red—maybe her songs were a bit ambitious for someone who wasn't a trained singer!

The pianist suggested I sing a Madonna song instead. Madonna's songs are also famous and iconic, but they have a simpler range and style that felt more approachable for a first-time singer.

I took a deep breath, chose one of her songs, and sang, putting all my effort into each note. I felt out of place and nervous, but I kept going, giving it everything I had.

To my surprise, I was offered the role! Although I didn't end up performing in the show, the experience taught me so much. At that time, I wasn't quite ready for such a big challenge or to take time away from my career with American Ballet Theatre. But the audition prepared me in ways I couldn't have imagined. Years later, I fully embraced the Broadway world as one of the leads in *On the Town*, playing Ivy Smith, a character who required me to sing, act, and dance. The lessons I learned from that first audition gave me the confidence to step outside my comfort zone and take on that new challenge.

Trying new things isn't about being perfect—it's about being brave enough to take a chance and learn along the way. Sometimes, stepping into something unfamiliar opens doors to new parts of yourself and helps you grow in ways you didn't expect. So if you ever get the chance to try something outside your comfort zone, take it. You might find that you're stronger and more capable than you ever thought. And even if it feels a little scary, remember that just trying is something to be proud of.

"Dear Misty, I decided to be in the talent show. I'm doing a comedy routine, but I'm scared nobody will laugh. I've never done anything onstage. Do you ever have stage fright? How do you deal with it? How do you deal with being embarrassed in public?"

Comedy takes a lot of courage, and the fact that you're willing to step onstage and make people laugh is already a huge accomplishment. Even though it's natural to wonder how the audience will react, especially when it's your first time, you're already doing something amazing by putting yourself out there.

While I don't experience stage fright exactly, I do get anxious before going onstage, especially when the stakes are high. I remember my first time performing the lead role in *Swan Lake*—one of the most iconic and technically demanding roles in ballet. There's so much history and expectation tied to it, and as the first Black woman to perform this role at ABT, I felt the weight of that moment. My mind was filled with what-ifs—*What if I make a mistake? What if I don't meet expectations? What if I don't feel ready?* But I reminded myself why I was there. Performing is something I love deeply, and once I stepped out onto the stage, those nerves began to fade.

When those preshow nerves kick in, I focus on my breathing. Deep breaths help me calm down and reconnect with why I'm there: to share something special with the audience. I also remind myself that it's okay if things don't go perfectly. Performing is about giving your all, not about being flawless.

And as for handling embarrassment—I've had plenty of awkward moments onstage! I've stumbled, forgotten steps, and even had costumes come undone! But I've learned that the audience often respects you more when you handle mistakes with grace. If something goes wrong, I try to smile and keep going. People remember your courage and effort, not the small slip-ups.

Take a deep breath, enjoy every moment, and remember why you're there. Even if things don't go exactly as planned, you're already winning by sharing your talent and making people smile. You might be surprised by how many people will be cheering you on!

stepping outside your comfort zone

Sometimes, the most meaningful growth happens when we step beyond what feels comfortable. For me, that moment came when I ventured into the apparel industry, driven by a need I experienced firsthand in my own career.

My first attempt at creating a dancewear line didn't succeed, but it became a valuable learning experience—like my "training" for the industry. That experience helped me recognize the challenges and prepared me for the next big opportunity: becoming an Under Armour Athlete. This partnership was a turning point—not just for me but for ballet as a whole. It brought ballet into the same conversation as sports like football and basketball, showcasing the incredible athleticism that dance requires. Under Armour also gave me the chance to design my own signature line, allowing me to address the gaps I'd noticed in the market and turn my vision into reality.

Now, as co-owner of Greatness Wins, I design athletic wear for people who take fitness seriously. This isn't just an athleisure line—it's created for those who are committed to working out consistently and want to look and feel great while doing it.

Stepping into this role took me far outside my comfort zone. I dealt with imposter syndrome, questioning if my ideas would resonate or if I could succeed in such a competitive industry. But ballet taught me an important lesson: Progress happens one step at a time. Each small effort builds toward something greater, and I leaned on that mindset to trust the process and keep moving forward.

What made my contributions unique was the perspective I brought as an athlete, artist, and consumer. As an athlete, I understood the physical demands of movement and the importance of clothing that supports performance. As an artist, I valued design and beauty, transforming functional pieces into something inspiring. And as a consumer, I recognized the gaps in the market—like the lack of options for curvier, athletic builds—and was determined to fill those voids with thoughtful, innovative designs.

This journey taught me that you don't need all the answers when starting something new. What matters most is your willingness to learn, adapt, and trust in the value of your unique experiences. By combining my perspective with hard work and determination, I turned setbacks into opportunities and created something meaningful. It's a lesson I hold on to with every new challenge—and one I hope encourages you to step confidently into your own unexplored paths.

"Dear Misty, I just started going to a new school, and I want to join the Dungeons & Dragons club. I don't think there are any girls in the club, though. What would you do?"

It can definitely be intimidating to step into a space where you might be the only girl. I've been in that situation many times throughout my life and career—often being one of the only, or even the only, Black person in the room. I know how uncomfortable that can feel at first, but I've also learned that stepping into those spaces can lead to incredible growth and inspiration—not just for others who see you there but for you, too.

I remember being a teenager and walking into a new ballet studio where I was the only Black girl in the class. I was so nervous, but the other dancers completely embraced me. What stood out most was how we all connected through our mutual love for the craft—ballet became the bridge that brought us together. Those moments reminded me that stepping into new spaces can open up unexpected friendships and opportunities.

When you follow your passion and put in the effort to be part of something new, it's hard, but it's also truly admirable. You're showing courage and strength, and that's powerful. Who knows? You might even inspire other girls to join the club someday because they saw you leading the way.

If D&D is something you're excited about, go for it! You belong there just as much as anyone else. Let your passion lead you, and remember that stepping into a new space can be a special experience that helps you grow and leaves a lasting impact on others.

"Dear Misty, I love ballet, just like you. I want to take lessons and maybe even be a professional dancer.

I'm worried about what people will say, because I'm a boy, but I'm trying not to let that stop me."

It's inspiring to hear how much you love ballet, and I want you to know that your passion for dance is something truly special. I've had the privilege of mentoring young boys just starting their ballet journeys, as well as young men in the middle of their training or professional careers. It's so admirable to see someone, especially at a young age, follow their passion, despite criticism or old-fashioned ideas about what boys should or shouldn't do.

Choosing ballet as a boy can come with challenges, but it also brings incredible rewards. Ballet will teach you so much more than technique—it's about discipline, resilience, confidence, and the courage to follow your heart. These are skills that will shape who you are for life, far beyond the studio or stage.

You're not alone, either. Some of the greatest ballet dancers in history were men who changed and enriched the art form. Dancers like Rudolf Nureyev, Mikhail Baryshnikov, and Carlos Acosta have left a lasting legacy, and contemporary dancers like Calvin Royal III and James B. Whiteside continue to inspire people around the world. You're part of a strong tradition of male dancers who have shown that ballet is about strength, grace, and passion—things that have nothing to do with gender.

Every time you step into the studio, you're building something meaningful—not just as a dancer, but as a person. Keep going, stay focused on what brings you joy, and know that your love for ballet is more powerful than any outdated stereotype. By pursuing it, you're already inspiring others and making a difference, even if you're just beginning your journey.

Finding Your People: Building a Support Network

Finding people who uplift and support you is one of the most important things you can do for yourself. As you go through life, you'll realize that surrounding yourself with a strong support network and genuine friends can make all the difference in how you navigate challenges and celebrate successes.

When I was seven, I joined the Boys & Girls Club of San Pedro, and it quickly became my second home. It was the first place where I found consistency and stability, something I hadn't had growing up due to my family's constant moving. At the club, I didn't feel judged for being shy or for the challenges I had faced. Instead, I was welcomed with open arms and encouraged to explore new experiences. It was also where I first understood the value of having a mentor—someone who believes in you, guides you, and helps you grow. That foundation shaped how I view the importance of community and support today.

It was also the place where I was introduced to ballet. This moment was a turning point for me—not just in terms of discovering my passion, but also in terms of finding my people. It took some time for me to build friendships, but as I grew more comfortable with who I was, I started to connect with people who shared similar interests and passions. These friendships were rooted in mutual respect, understanding, and support, and they helped me feel more at ease with myself.

As I progressed in my ballet career, I realized just how important it was to have a community around me. Ballet can be incredibly demanding, both physically and emotionally, and having people who genuinely support you through all the ups and downs is invaluable. Whether it was the bonds I shared with my fellow dancers, my mentors, or my close friends, these relationships became my backbone.

These people helped me stay grounded, encouraged me to keep going when things got tough, and celebrated with me when I achieved my goals.

I want to emphasize that finding your people is about more than just having friends—it's about building a network of individuals who believe in you, who understand you, and who are there for you no matter what. These are the people who will lift you up when you're feeling down, who will cheer you on when you're chasing your dreams, and who will stand by your side through all of life's challenges.

It's also important to remember that building these relationships takes time. You may not find your people right away, and that's okay. Focus on being yourself, pursuing your passions, and being open to the connections that come your way. Over time, you'll find the friends and mentors who truly get you, who accept you for who you are, and who will be there to support you every step of the way.

As you go through life, remember to prioritize building a support network that celebrates who you are. Seek out friendships that are rooted in respect and understanding and surround yourself with people who believe in you and your dreams. These relationships will be some of the most valuable and meaningful parts of your journey.

"Dear Misty, my best friend and I both tried out for the school play, and I got the bigger part. He says he's happy for me, but I can tell he's upset. Have you ever had to compete with a friend? How did you keep things cool between you?"

I really understand how you're feeling because I've been in a similar situation. When I was in middle school, I auditioned for the drill team and had to compete against my friend for the position of captain. It was difficult because I was so focused on achieving my own goals, but I also wanted her to succeed. In the end, I was named captain, and she became cocaptain, and what's amazing is that the experience actually brought us closer! We found a way to support each other and share in the success together.

What I learned in that situation—and what I think can help you—is the importance of fostering healthy communication and *being* a good friend, even when competition is involved. It's natural to feel a mix of emotions, and your friend might feel disappointed even if he's happy for you. The key is to talk openly with him. Saying something like "I'm really excited about this role, but I know it's tough when things don't go as hoped. I'm here for you no matter what" opens the door for an honest conversation where both of you feel seen and understood.

One thing I realized is that you don't have to lose or let go of people when situations like this come up. Instead, these moments can strengthen your bond. By communicating openly and supporting each other, you don't lose your friendship—in fact, you can deepen it. Being a good friend doesn't mean downplaying your success. You can celebrate your own achievements and still be there for your friend. I've found that when you lift each other up, it makes both of you stronger.

This is just one moment in both of your journeys. There will be many more opportunities ahead, and by sticking together and supporting each other, you will make your friendship even stronger. With empathy and communication, you and your friend can come out of this closer than ever.

"Dear Misty, I have a mentor who helps me with school, but I'm afraid of disappointing them. Did you ever feel like that with your mentors? How did you deal with it?"

I've put a lot of responsibility on myself throughout my life because I care deeply about what I do, and I know how much my mentors have poured into me. There were times when I felt like I had to be perfect, because I didn't want to let them down or waste the effort they'd invested in me. I thought there was no room for mistakes.

I've learned that even though I held myself to these high standards, my mentors weren't expecting perfection. In fact, now that I'm a mentor myself, I realize how much we as mentors actually learn from those we're guiding. It's not a one-way street. Just as your mentor is giving you support, they're also learning about you and your journey, and they're even discovering more about themselves through the process. They get just as much out of mentoring as they're giving.

Rather than focusing on being perfect, think about the growth you're both experiencing. Your mentors are there to help you learn and grow—they don't expect you to have it all figured out. And every step you take—be it a success or a lesson learned—helps both you and your mentor become better.

Finding other ways to express yourself

Self-expression is a big part of what makes us human. It's how we share who we are, especially when words aren't enough. For me, ballet became my first way to truly express myself. Initially, I focused on mastering the steps, learning every move with precision. But as I grew as a dancer, I realized ballet was more than just technique—it was a language. It allowed me to share emotions and tell stories without speaking, making me feel free and understood.

Of course, there were challenges. Ballet takes years of discipline, and there were times when I doubted if I'd ever find my true voice in it. But those moments taught me resilience and showed me that self-expression isn't always easy—it's something you grow into.

As I got older, I found new ways to express myself. Cooking was one of the first. When I moved to New York at seventeen to dance, I had to learn to cook just to take care of myself. Over time, I realized cooking could be creative, too—a way to relax, show care, and express myself without words. It wasn't always smooth—I've burned plenty of meals—but even the mistakes became part of the story. Each dish was a way to share comfort and creativity.

Writing came next. I started journaling in middle school, but publishing books took self-expression to a new level. Journaling had been a private way to reflect on my thoughts, but sharing my story with others was both exciting and a little scary. Writing opened up a new avenue for me to open up to people in a way I couldn't onstage, allowing me to share my journey and emotions with the world.

Self-expression can take many forms. It's a way to process and share emotions—from fear and sadness to anger, happiness, or excitement. Ballet lets me show grace and strength, cooking allows me to share care and creativity, and writing helps me process my thoughts and connect with others.

There's no single right way to express yourself. It could be through art, words, food, or ideas—whatever helps you feel in tune with yourself and the world around you. Don't be afraid to explore. Through painting, playing an instrument, or trying something totally new, let your voice shine in whatever way feels right for you.

"Dear Misty, I have a lot going on at home and at school. A lot of the time I feel sad, upset, or pretty angry. I need to find a way to deal with my feelings that doesn't involve yelling at people, slamming things, or crying in my room. What do you do when you have big feelings?"

Thank you for being so honest and brave in sharing how you feel. I know what it's like to have a lot going on at home and at school, and to feel like the emotions are just too much to handle. When I was younger, I didn't always have the support or tools to deal with those big feelings. I often shut down and held everything inside, which sometimes led to migraines or moments when I would explode at my siblings. Looking back, I wish I had known some of the strategies I use now to manage those emotions in a healthier way.

One thing I've found helpful is writing down my thoughts and feelings. When I started writing, my journal became a place where I could let out whatever I was feeling without holding back. Putting my emotions into words helped me understand them better and made me feel like I wasn't carrying all that weight alone. Even just a few sentences can make a difference—it's like giving those feelings somewhere to go.

I also learned that moving my body helps when the emotions feel too big. For me, dance became a powerful way to release stress and express myself. But you don't need to be a dancer to benefit from movement. Taking a walk, stretching, or even jumping around to your favorite song can help clear your mind and release some of that built-up energy.

Finally, I wish I had known how important it is to talk to someone you trust. Talking to a friend, family member, or teacher about what's going on inside can be really freeing.

Even just saying "I'm feeling overwhelmed" out loud can help ease the tension.

Remember, it's okay to feel sad, upset, or angry sometimes. What's important is finding ways to express and release those feelings so they don't take over. Be patient with yourself, take deep breaths, and know that it's brave to seek out healthy ways to manage your emotions.

> *"Dear Misty, I feel like I'm always stressed out about homework, tests, and keeping up with my friends. what do you do when everything feels too overwhelming?"*

I understand how overwhelming it can be when everything seems to pile up at once. Homework, tests, friendship . . . it's a lot to manage! When I was your age, I often felt that same stress, especially when I was balancing school and dance. It's not easy, but I want to share a few things that help me when everything feels like too much.

First, take a moment to pause and breathe. It might sound simple, but taking deep, calming breaths can help your mind and body feel more at ease. When I'm feeling overwhelmed, I close my eyes, take a few slow, deep breaths, and remind myself that it's okay to take things one step at a time.

Another thing that really helps is making a list or plan. When you're juggling so much, breaking things down into smaller, manageable pieces can make everything feel less intimidating. Prioritize what needs to be done first and set realistic goals for yourself. Even crossing off one small task can give you a sense of accomplishment and reduce stress.

And don't forget to take breaks and be kind to yourself. Sometimes, when we're so focused on getting everything done, we forget that it's okay to step away for a little while. Listen to your favorite song, stretch, or go on a walk—taking a short break can make a big difference in how you feel.

Remember, you're doing the best you can, and it's okay to ask for help or take a moment to rest. Being kind to yourself and knowing that it's okay not to be perfect all the time is so important.

Turning setbacks into Fuel

Big dreams often come with challenges, and my journey has been no exception. One of the most important lessons I've learned is that setbacks don't define you—they help you grow.

Before my partnership with Under Armour, I set out to create a dancewear line on my own. My vision was clear: vibrant, fashion-forward colors like deep teal and dusty amethyst, and dancewear designed for plus-size and athletic builds, offering real bust support instead of the basic linings typical in leotards. I wanted to celebrate all body types while meeting practical needs.

Despite my passion, I lacked business experience and the right team to make it happen. I took on too much, and the project didn't go as planned. Watching something I cared so much about fall short was difficult, leaving me disappointed and frustrated.

But that experience taught me a critical lesson: Resilience isn't about avoiding setbacks; it's about how you respond. Instead of giving up, I reflected on what went wrong and learned from it. Mistakes are part of the process, and each one helps you grow stronger. I realized the importance of starting with a solid foundation—having the right team, taking time to learn the basics, and pacing myself. These lessons set me up for success when I later partnered with Under Armour and cofounded Greatness Wins.

Taking care of yourself is a big part of building resilience. Pause to think things over, reach out to friends, or remind yourself why you started—engaging in self-care helps you stay strong. When we look after ourselves, we build the strength to lift others up too.

This idea is a big part of why I started the Misty Copeland Foundation. Through the foundation, I share the lessons I've learned from ballet, like how to stay disciplined and keep going even in the face of adversity, with young people facing their own challenges. The foundation isn't just about dance; it's about building confidence and the courage to push through setbacks. I want young dancers to know that every challenge they face helps shape who they're becoming, preparing them for an even brighter future.

By turning challenges into opportunities, you grow stronger and inspire others to do the same. Every setback is a step forward, and your perseverance can encourage those around you to keep reaching for their dreams.

"Dear Misty, I know you do a lot to help other people. I need to do some volunteering or public service as part of school, but I don't know where to start. How did you get started, and how can I find a way to make a difference?"

Thank you so much for reaching out and for wanting to make a difference; it's truly a wonderful way to grow and learn more about yourself while helping others. I'm so excited for you to start this journey!

When I think about where I began, it all started with the community that surrounded me as a young girl. The Boys & Girls Club played a huge role in my life—it's where I took my very first ballet class. That experience not only sparked my love for dance but also showed me the importance of having opportunities and supportive spaces. Now, as an ambassador for the Boys & Girls Club, I give back to an organization that built me up when I needed it most.

For me, acts of service have always been tied to resilience. Life is full of challenges, and sometimes we need to hold on to the things that make us stronger, whether that's art, community, or simply helping someone else. Volunteering is an act of resilience, because it reminds us that we can uplift others even as we face our own struggles.

To start finding your path in service, think about what matters most to you. What brings you joy or piques your curiosity? Do you enjoy working with younger kids, helping in community centers, being around animals, or lending a hand at local events? Speak to teachers, friends, or family members; they might know of opportunities where you can make a difference. Community centers, libraries, after-school programs, and shelters are all great places to begin.

Remember, acts of service don't have to be grand to be meaningful. Small acts, like helping an elderly neighbor carry groceries or spending time with someone who needs company, can create powerful ripples—positive effects that spread far beyond the moment, touching more lives than you might realize. It's these moments that teach us resilience, empathy, and strength.

Volunteering shapes who you are and how you view the world. And who knows? You might find something that sparks a lifelong passion, just as I did with dance when I first walked into the Boys & Girls Club. Take your time, stay open, and know that each step you take—no matter how small—is a testament to your strength and your willingness to grow.

"Dear Misty, how do you stay motivated to help others, even when you're going through tough times yourself?"

Staying motivated to help others, even during tough times, is not always easy, but it is one of the most powerful things we can do for ourselves and our communities. For me, inner strength and helping others are closely connected.

There have been moments in my life when I felt overwhelmed by challenges—like the physical demands of ballet, personal setbacks, or periods of doubt. During those times, turning my focus outward and helping others brought me a sense of purpose and reminded me why I pushed through difficult times in the first place. Giving back, especially during tough times, connects us to the people around us and reinforces that we are not alone.

I've learned that resilience isn't just about enduring rough times; it's about finding ways to rise above them. Helping others has always been a source of strength for me because it shifts my focus from what I'm experiencing to what I can do for someone else. I remember times at school when I felt uncertain and often isolated, not having many friends. But being there for someone who was facing even bigger challenges helped put things into perspective. Reaching out reminded me that even if I felt alone, I could still make a difference for someone else—and that gave me a sense of connection and purpose.

When you find yourself in tough times, look for small ways to help someone else, even if they're as simple as listening to a friend or offering a helping hand. These acts can renew your spirit and remind you that we are all stronger when we lift each other up.

Remember that helping others isn't just about what you give; it's also about what you receive—a renewed sense of hope, connection, and resilience that will carry you through whatever comes your way.

FIFTH POSITION

"assemblé"–put it all together

IN BALLET, ASSEMBLÉ (AH–SAHM–BLAY)
means "assembled" or "joined together." It is a graceful
movement where a dancer sweeps one foot into the air,
jumps, and lands with both feet together in fifth position.

Similarly, life encourages us to assemble our knowledge,
experiences, and lessons to create something complete and
meaningful. When we do this—onstage or in life—we can
land exactly where we want to be, confident and steady.

Dear Reader,

In ballet, assemblé *means to bring things
together in harmony. In life, it's about combining*

everything you've learned to create a steady, confident path forward. I've realized that no matter how much we know, there's always room to learn, adapt, and grow. Life's challenges shape us, helping us refine what we already know and discover new ways to thrive.

Reflecting on your experiences and blending advice from others with your own insights is like making a favorite recipe. The key ingredients—like trust, effort, and kindness—are always there, but you can add your unique touch. Sometimes, things will turn out just right; other times, they might not. That's okay! Every step teaches you something valuable.

Now that we've explored so much together, let's think about how you can create your own "life recipe."

I'll share some ideas and activities that bring me joy and balance, and I hope they inspire you to build a life that's truly yours.

In this section, I'll share some of my routines, practices, and favorite things to help you reflect and build on each of the four positions we've explored together in this book: "First Position: 'Attitude'—Love Yourself First," "Second Position: 'Développé'—Discover Yourself," "Third Position: 'Relevé'—Rise Above Challenges," and "Fourth Position: 'Grand Jeté'—Take the Leap." Along the way, you'll find "Pas de Deux Prompts"—pas de deux (pah-duh-DEW) means "step of two"— which invite you to try the activities along with me. These prompts are your chance to leap into your best life, combining all you've learned to discover and fully realize your own unique path.

Let's take this final step together—one assemblé at a time!

A Recipe for My Ideal Day

In ballet, every movement comes together to create something harmonious and beautiful, much like the way we assemble moments in our daily lives. It's not about chasing perfection but about savoring the small, meaningful pieces that bring joy, balance, and growth.

In the first chapter of this book, we explored the importance of attitude and the role of self-love in living a fulfilling life. Loving yourself and keeping a positive mindset starts with prioritizing your needs, practicing self-care, and doing things that feel right to you. For me, an ideal day feels like a well-loved recipe, blending connection, creativity, and care into something truly fulfilling. Here's how I put it all together:

My Key Ingredients

1 generous cup of morning journaling and gratitude

2 scoops of play, dance, or music time with my son

A dash of cooking something fun together

1 scoop of a dance or cardio class

A heaping tablespoon of laughter with friends and family

1 hour of uninterrupted quiet time

A sprinkle of spontaneous joy—watching a movie or singing along to favorite songs

A dash of creativity—writing or painting

A pinch of TV or a cozy read before bed, wrapping up with gratitude

Each of these moments adds up to something that energizes and centers me. Blending in flexibility and kindness makes each day unique, reminding me that happiness often comes from the simplest pleasures.

pas de Deux prompt:
Make Your Own recipe for a great Day

What would make your day truly special? Think about the things that fill you with joy, help you feel balanced, or bring a smile to your face. Maybe you like spending time with friends, boosting your mood with a creative project, or enjoying a peaceful moment just for yourself.

Your recipe for an ideal day can be a mix of fun, quiet, creativity, and connection—whatever makes you feel like the best version of yourself. Take a moment to imagine it and think about how you can make it happen!

My Favorite recipe: simple Banana Pancakes

In my ideal day, I always include a dash of cooking something fun with my family. It's one of the ways we connect, share joy, and create special memories. This recipe for banana pancakes is a family favorite—not just because it's delicious, but because it brings us together in such a meaningful way.

The real magic lies in the time spent making them together. My son, Jackson, who's a toddler, loves to help mash the bananas and mix the batter, and his enthusiasm turns the process into a cherished ritual. These moments are more than just cooking—they're opportunities to share laughter, teamwork, and a sense of warmth that brings us closer.

It's not just about the pancakes; it's about creating lasting memories and celebrating the joy of being together. Let's whip up some magic!

The recipe should be done with adult supervision.

What You Need
1 ripe banana
1 egg

How to Make It
Mash the banana in a bowl until smooth.
Crack the egg into the bowl and mix until fully combined.
Heat a nonstick pan over medium heat.
Pour small amounts of batter into the pan and cook 1–2 minutes on each side or until golden brown.
Serve warm and enjoy!

Tips for Living Your Best Life

To live your best life, start with what you've already learned about yourself. In "First Position: 'Attitude'—Love Yourself First," we talked about attitude and the importance of loving yourself first. This chapter builds on that idea by reminding us that each of us is unique—and our idea of a "best life" will be different from someone else's. Reflect on who you are, what's important to you, and what you enjoy. Loving yourself means embracing those differences and finding what makes you feel whole, happy, and cared for.

Here are some ideas to help you feel connected, balanced, and fulfilled every day:

Make Time for Friends and Family: Spend time with people who uplift you. Planning movie nights, catching up over a quick call, or having spontaneous hangouts—those moments matter. I have a small circle of close friends, and it feels meaningful just relaxing together. Sometimes, a friend might say, "I'm nearby, want to meet up?" Those simple moments can bring so much comfort and joy. Laughing and sharing stories creates a sense of connection and support.

Practice Self-Acceptance: Embrace your quirks and strengths. I struggled with self-acceptance for years, but gradually I came to understand how much supportive friendships have contributed to my growth. Having people who truly see and accept me allowed me to become more confident and at peace with who I am.

Stay Open-Minded: Approach life with curiosity and a willingness to grow. Being open-minded wasn't something that came naturally to me—I grew up seeing change as risky and uncomfortable. Over time, with the encouragement of my husband and others in my support system, I began to view change as a way to grow. Now, staying open and positive is something I practice every day, and it has strengthened my resilience and opened up new possibilities in my life.

Make Time for Fun: Life is about balance. When I was growing up, survival often took priority, and fun wasn't always part of the plan. Even as a ballerina, the intense demands of training left little space for anything else. But I've learned how essential it is to carve out moments of joy. Be it an impromptu dance, cooking with my family, or simply sharing a laugh, I now make time for what fills my heart and keeps life light.

Finding Joy in the Little Things

Happiness doesn't always come from big moments—it's often found in the little things we do or notice every day. For me, joy comes from the simple, silly, or special moments that make life brighter. These are the things that bring a

smile to my face, lift my spirits, and remind me to appreciate what's around me.

My Ten Happy Things

Dancing around the house to my favorite music

Movie nights with popcorn

Singing along to good music really loud

Warm blankets on a chilly day

Getting a hug from someone I love

Waking up and realizing it's Saturday

Making up silly dances with my son and husband

The first bite of pizza

Wearing fuzzy socks on a cold day

Lying on a blanket and watching the clouds drift by

PAS DE DEUX PROMPT:
YOUR HAPPY THINGS

*What makes you happy? Think of three things that bring
you joy, no matter how big or small. Write them down
and reflect on why they make you feel good. How can you
include more of those moments in your day?*

*Happiness is all around us—we just have to take the
time to notice it!*

Building Happiness: My Favorite Things

In "Second Position: 'Développé'—Discover Yourself," we talked about figuring out who you truly are and growing into the person you're meant to be. Life is an adventure, and along the way, you gather experiences, hobbies, and memories that shape you. The things you love now might change as you grow, but that's part of what makes life so exciting—every new discovery adds to your invisible "back-pack" of things that make you *you.*

Happiness isn't the same for everyone, and that's what makes it so special. It's about finding the moments, activities, and people that bring you joy, balance, and comfort. A song that lifts your mood, a book that inspires you, or a snack that makes everything feel better—each favorite thing helps you understand yourself a little more.

In this section, I invite you to explore with me! Building a playlist, finding a new way to take care of yourself, or writing about what makes you happiest—this is your chance to discover what brings you joy.

Grab a journal, a piece of paper, or even just a quiet moment to think. Let's take this next step in finding joy and building happiness, one favorite thing at a time.

My Playlist

Here are some of my favorite songs that lift me up, calm me down, or help me focus. Music can be powerful—it's like a friend that matches your energy or lifts your spirits when you need it most! I've included songs for different moods: "power-up" songs for confidence, calming tracks for focus, and joyful tunes for pure happiness.

Mariah Carey, "Make It Happen"

An empowering anthem: Sometimes, we all need a reminder of how strong we really are. Mariah Carey's "Make It Happen" inspires me to believe in myself and stay determined, even when things get tough. It's a powerful song that energizes me and reinforces that with hard work and confidence, I can overcome challenges and achieve my dreams.

Wolfgang Amadeus Mozart, Piano Concerto No. 23 in A Major, K. 488, Second Movement

A soothing classical piece: Classical music helps me slow down and focus, especially when life feels overwhelming. The second movement of Mozart's Piano Concerto No. 23 in A Major, K. 488, is one of my favorites. Its soft, beautiful melody calms my mind and reminds me of the strength found in still-ness, helping me feel grounded and ready to move forward.

Bruno Mars, "24K Magic"

An uplifting pop song: Sometimes, all it takes is a fun song to turn my day around. Bruno Mars's "24K Magic" always lifts my spirits—it's upbeat, catchy, and impossible not to dance to! Whenever I hear it, I can't help but smile and let go of any stress. Songs like this remind me to embrace joy, have fun, and enjoy life's lighthearted moments.

Lauryn Hill, "Ex-Factor"

An inspirational ballad: A great ballad can speak straight to your heart. Lauryn Hill's "Ex-Factor" is one of those songs for me—it's soulful and emotional, and it reminds me of the strength that comes from being honest with yourself. Listening to it inspires me to stay resilient and keep moving forward, no matter how tough things get. It's a reminder that growth often comes through life's challenges.

Kamasi Washington, "Clair de Lune"

Jazz fusion: Jazz fusion feels like pure musical freedom to me. Kamasi Washington's "Claire de Lune" catches my attention because it reimagines a classical piece with fresh, modern sounds. Listening to it inspires me to think creatively and shows how blending different styles can create something truly unique and powerful.

H.E.R., "FOCUS"

R & B vibes: R & B has a special way of pulling you in with its smooth melodies and heartfelt lyrics. H.E.R.'s "Focus" is one of my favorites—it's soulful and reminds me to pause, reflect, and stay connected to my emotions. R & B inspires me to express myself and appreciate the rhythm of life, helping me stay grounded and in tune with what truly matters.

Kendrick Lamar, "Alright"

Hip-hop energy: Hip-hop is all about confidence, rhythm, and telling your story. Kendrick Lamar's "Alright" is one of those songs that fills me with energy and hope. Its bold beats and powerful lyrics remind me to stay strong and keep going. Hip-hop inspires me to believe in myself and shows how music can motivate, uplift, and give you the confidence to face any challenge.

Kings of Leon, "Use Somebody"

Alternative rhythms: Alternative songs often surprise me

with their unique melodies and emotional depth. Kings of Leon's "Use Somebody" really resonates with me—it's both powerful and reflective, making me think about connection and the support we need to grow. This genre reminds me that stepping outside what feels familiar can spark creativity, inspire new ideas, and open my mind to fresh perspectives.

NO DOUbt, "Just a Girl"

Rock power: Rock music has a way of making me feel bold and unstoppable. No Doubt's "Just a Girl" stands out because it's all about empowerment and finding your strength. Its energetic beat and fearless lyrics remind me to embrace who I am and never back down from a challenge. Rock songs like this inspire confidence and courage, giving me the motivation to keep moving forward, no matter what.

Lucky Daye, "Roll Some Mo"

Neo-soul bliss: Neo-soul is like a deep breath for my emotions—calm, inspiring, and full of feeling. Lucky Daye's "Roll Some Mo" is a perfect example. Its smooth vocals and steady rhythm remind me to slow down and enjoy life's little moments. Listening to this kind of music helps me reset, clear my mind, and find a fresh perspective, even on the busiest days.

Pas de Deux Prompt:
Make Your Own Playlist

What music helps you feel relaxed or energized? Create your own playlist and discover how music affects your mood. You might learn songs that make you feel confident, calm, or simply happy. Write down your favorite songs and note how they make you feel. Then listen to them whenever you need a boost! Grab your favorite device or a piece of paper and start exploring the music that moves you. Music has a wonderful way of expressing our feelings and can be a great companion through all life's moments. Happy listening!

Stories to Read and Treasure

Books are like mirrors and windows—they reflect our experiences while opening us up to new worlds. Like the *développé* in ballet, stories help us grow, unfolding our unique selves with patience and courage.

In "Second Position: 'Développé'—Discover Yourself," we explored the importance of challenging yourself and stepping outside your comfort zone. Each book I've chosen connects to that journey, celebrating resilience, creativity, and bravery.

I hope these stories inspire you to dream, face challenges with strength, and embrace your unique path. Let them take you on unforgettable adventures and remind you that every step forward is part of becoming who you're meant to be.

Brave Ballerina: The Story of Janet Collins, by Michelle Meadows

Janet Collins was the first Black prima ballerina to perform at the Metropolitan Opera, and her story of determination and grace inspires me deeply. She paved the way for dancers like me, breaking barriers and showing what's possible with courage and resilience.

Call Us What We Carry: Poems, by Amanda Gorman

Amanda Gorman's words are so powerful—they reflect history, strength, and healing in a way that moves and inspires me. Like Amanda, I believe art has the power to create change, celebrate who we are, and help us overcome challenges.

Finding Langston, by Lesa Cline-Ransome

Langston's discovery of poetry and self-expression reminds me of my own journey with dance. Both of us found creative outlets that gave us strength and purpose, and this book beautifully shows how art can heal and inspire.

Taking Flight: From war orphan to star Ballerina, by Michaela DePrince

Michaela DePrince was not only an incredible talent but also a dear friend. Her journey from an orphan in Sierra Leone to a world-renowned ballerina is a story of determination, courage, and hope. Michaela's determination to rise above her circumstances and pursue her dreams inspires all of us to dream big and embrace the transformative power of art.

The Year we Fell from space, by Amy Sarig King

This story about a young girl finding her strength through stargazing and art reminds me of the power of creativity to help us heal and grow. Like the main character, I've faced moments when life felt overwhelming, but I found comfort and clarity through dance and self-expression. This book beautifully shows how turning to something you love can help you navigate life's challenges and find hope.

Finding Your calm

In "Third Position: 'Relevé'—Rise Above Challenges," we talked about rising above life's obstacles with resilience and grace. Every time you face a challenge and rise above it, you grow stronger and more confident in who you are.

But to overcome challenges, you also need to take care of your mind and body. Finding your calm doesn't have to be hard. In fact, it's often the little things—like taking a deep breath, moving your body, or doing something you love—that make the biggest difference.

I've learned that even small moments of reflection or joy can help me feel balanced and ready to take on the day. Just like ballet, where each step builds toward something greater, these simple wellness tips can help you recharge, refocus, and keep moving forward. Let's explore how you can find your calm and lift yourself up, one small step at a time.

My Path to Balance

Stretch it out: Take five minutes to stretch your body, with a full-body stretch or just by rolling your neck and shoulders. It helps release tension and improves circulation.

> ### pas de Deux prompt
> *Try this with me—stand up and stretch along with your favorite calming music. How does your body feel afterward?*

Find your breath: Pause and take ten deep breaths, focusing on the rise and fall of your chest. It's a quick way to feel grounded and calm.

> PAS DE DEUX PROMPT
> *Join me in a mini breathing session. Write down how you feel before and after.*

Step outside: Take a five-minute walk or simply stand in the sun and breathe in some fresh air. Nature has a way of resetting your mind.

> PAS DE DEUX PROMPT
> *Head outside for a few minutes. Can you spot something beautiful, like a flower, a bird, or the color of the sky?*

Turn on the tunes: Play your favorite song and have a quick dance break. Moving to music is a joyful way to shake off stress.

> PAS DE DEUX PROMPT
> *Dance along to a song you love. Write down how it made you feel—lighter, energized, or happier?*

Sip something soothing: Make yourself a calming drink, like herbal tea. Take a moment to sit quietly and enjoy it.

> ### pas de deux prompt
> *Try making a calming drink and savoring it slowly. What flavors and feelings stand out?*

Create something small: Doodle, write a few lines in a journal, or make a quick DIY craft. Expressing yourself creatively can clear your mind.

> ### pas de deux prompt
> *Create a quick doodle or jot down your thoughts. What do you feel inspired by?*

Unplug for a bit: Put your phone on airplane mode for ten minutes and focus on being present, regardless of if you're reading, cooking, or just relaxing.

> ### pas de deux prompt
> *Try unplugging with me. How does it feel to step away from your screen for a little while?*

Tidy a small space: Organize your desk or clean out a drawer. A little tidying can give you a sense of accomplishment and clarity.

> PAS de DEUX Prompt
> *Pick one spot to tidy. How does the space feel once it's refreshed?*

Gratitude pause: Write down three things you're grateful for in this moment, no matter how small. Gratitude helps shift your mindset to the positive.

> PAS de DEUX Prompt
> *Take a gratitude pause with me. What three things are bringing you joy right now?*

Laugh it out: Watch a funny video, share a joke with a friend, or think of something that always makes you smile. Laughter is a natural stress reliever.

> PAS de DEUX Prompt
> *Share a laugh with me. What's something that always makes you giggle?*

My Simple Ways to Feel Your Best

Taking care of yourself doesn't have to be difficult—it can actually be fun and simple! Here are three healthy snacks I love and three easy exercises or stretches that help me feel invigorated and balanced.

Favorite Healthy snacks

1. Edamame: Steamed edamame sprinkled with a bit of sea salt, perfect for a quick, healthy boost.
2. Pretzels with hummus: A crunchy, savory combo that's both satisfying and energizing.
3. Frozen grapes: A simple and refreshing snack, especially on a hot day.

Quick and Easy Exercises/stretches

1. Butterfly Stretch

The butterfly stretch is a simple way to loosen tight hips and improve flexibility. Sit on the floor, press the soles of your feet together, and let your knees naturally fall toward the ground. For a deeper stretch, gently press your knees down with your hands.

> ### pas de deux prompt
> *Hold the stretch for ten to fifteen seconds and focus on your breathing. Can you feel your hips and legs relaxing with each breath?*

2. Five-Minute Dance Party

Moving freely is an amazing way to recharge and have fun! A quick dance party is perfect for shaking off stress and boosting your mood. Put on a song you love and move however you feel—there's no wrong way to dance!

> ### pas de deux prompt
> *Choose your favorite upbeat song, press play, and let loose. How do you feel after moving and having fun?*

3. Leg Swings

Did you know this simple movement is also a ballet step? It's called *balançoire* (*bah-lahn-SWAR*), and it's all about rhythm and flow. Stand on one foot and gently swing the other leg forward and backward like a pendulum. Switch legs to keep it balanced.

> ### Pas de Deux Prompt
> *Choose your favorite upbeat song, press play, and let loose. How do you feel after moving and having fun?*

Mindful Moments

Find a quiet space, play a calming song, and close your eyes. Breathe in deeply, filling yourself with light, and exhale any tension. After a few minutes, reflect: How do you feel after taking this moment to pause and breathe?

My Five Golden Rules

Embrace the Journey

Success is not just about reaching the goal; it's about appreciating every step along the way. Challenges help you grow stronger.

> ### Pas de Deux Prompt
> *Write about a time when a challenge helped you learn or grow. How did it shape you?*

Stay True to Yourself

Authenticity is your superpower. Be proud of who you are and embrace your uniqueness.

> ### pas de deux prompt
> *Write down one thing that makes you uniquely you and how it helps you shine.*

Lift Others Up

Success is even sweeter when you bring others along. Kindness and support create a stronger community.

> ### pas de deux prompt
> *Write about a time when someone helped you or when you helped someone else. How did it feel?*

Stay Open to New Possibilities

Growth happens when you step outside your comfort zone. Be curious and welcome new experiences.

> ### pas de deux prompt
> *Think of one new thing you want to try. What excites you about it?*

Use Your Voice

Don't be afraid to speak up for yourself and others. Your voice is powerful and can inspire change.

> ### pas de Deux prompt
> *Think of something important to you. How would you express it to inspire others?*

make Every Day count

No two days are ever the same. Some feel magical, the kind we wish we could relive forever. Others bring challenges that push us to reflect and grow. And then there are quieter, ordinary days that may seem unremarkable but still play an important part in shaping who we are.

In "Fourth Position: 'Grand Jeté'—Take the Leap," we explored how stepping outside your comfort zone, discovering creativity, and expressing yourself can help you grow. Each day is an opportunity to practice these ideas—by trying something new, staying resilient in the face of challenges, or sharing kindness with others.

Taking time to reflect on your day can help you learn and grow. What brought you joy? How did you handle a challenge? What would you like to do differently tomorrow? These small reflections can show you how to live with more purpose and creativity while embracing the courage to step beyond what feels comfortable.

Here are some moments from my life that have shaped

who I am—times that challenged me, sparked my creativity, and reminded me of the importance of every kind of day. I hope they inspire you to reflect on your own journey and take bold steps toward building a life you love. Every day is a new chance to grow, learn, and create something meaningful!

A Typical Workday

My workdays are a blend of family time, creativity, and professional commitments, with each part bringing a strong sense of purpose. While ballet remains central to who I am, I've taken a step back from performing for now to focus on my family and explore new professional endeavors.

6:30 a.m.: My mornings begin when my son, Jackson, wakes up. We start the day playing together, I make his breakfast, and by nine a.m., I've dropped him off at school and am ready to focus on my own responsibilities.

10:00 a.m.: Once I'm back home, I might take a floor barre class to keep my body active and connected to movement. It's a grounding way to start a busy day. Afterward, I dive into Zoom meetings for my production company, collaborating with my team to bring exciting projects to life.

12:00 p.m.: Around lunchtime, I'll meet with my

manager, agent, and publicist to discuss opportunities and upcoming ideas.

1:00–5:00 p.m.: Afternoons are a blend of creativity and focus. I dedicate time to writing for my upcoming books—a process that allows me to reflect and share meaningful stories. Later in the day, I head to the Misty Copeland Foundation offices for meetings about expanding access to the arts and creating opportunities for young dancers.

5:00 p.m. onward: Evenings are equally full but take on a different energy. I make dinner for my family, enjoying those moments to connect and unwind together. Some nights, I head to an event or gala, representing causes I care about or celebrating the work of others.

Through it all, balance is the key. When I'm spending time with my family, collaborating on projects, or finding space for creativity, I aim to bring focus and joy to every part of the day.

A Typical Relaxed and Fun Day

Sometimes, it's important to have a day that's all about unwinding—unplugging from the usual rush and focusing on enjoying the moment. Even on these relaxing days, my mornings still start early—around six thirty a.m.—since Jackson wakes up bright and ready to go, weekend or not!

We usually start the day with playtime or a trip to the park. The fresh air and simple fun set the tone for an easygoing morning. Afterward, we'll treat ourselves to breakfast out as a family, savoring a slow start to the day.

Back at home, I might recharge with a quick nap or join a Pilates or ballet class to move my body and feel centered. In the afternoon, I love doing something creative with Jackson, like visiting a museum or seeing a show that sparks his imagination. These moments of exploration and curiosity make the day feel special, and we might wrap it up with a long walk home, reflecting on everything we enjoyed.

Evenings are all about family time. Jackson often joins me in the kitchen as my little sous chef, and we cook dinner together while listening to music. These simple moments— stirring batter, singing along to a favorite song—are some of my most cherished. After dinner, once Jackson is asleep, my husband and I unwind with a movie in bed and some popcorn. It's the perfect way to end a day that feels light, joyful, and balanced.

A Day I'd Do Differently: Learning from Challenges

Stretching myself too thin is usually what turns a good day into a stressful one. I'll never forget a day when I was dancing with ABT and preparing for an important dress rehearsal for a new role. I was so overwhelmed trying to do it all that I misread the schedule. I thought I had plenty of time to prepare, so I decided to take a private ballet class to feel even more ready. But when I arrived at the theater, I found out I was five minutes away from making my first entrance—and I wasn't even in costume.

What I've always been good at is jumping in, being present, and committing fully to the moment. Somehow, I managed to pull myself together and get through the rehearsal. But afterward, I couldn't help but replay it in my mind. I kept asking myself: If I'd been on time, would my rehearsal—and ultimately my performance—have gone better?

Looking back, I realize that moment taught me an important lesson about setting boundaries and respecting my limits. It's natural to try to do everything, but sometimes less is more. I learned to prioritize what truly matters and let go of trying to overprepare. And while it's hard not to beat yourself up, I've also realized that others probably moved on from that moment much faster than I did!

One of My Best Days Ever: Celebrating Joy

One of the most unforgettable nights of my life was the last time I performed *Swan Lake*. At the time, I didn't know it would be my final performance of the role, but it holds an incredibly special place in my heart. A year earlier, I had started training with a new teacher, motivated by my desire to feel more comfortable in the role of Odette/Odile. The journey wasn't easy—I had several performances that year that didn't go as well as I'd hoped, and the pressure was intense. *Swan Lake* is one of the most iconic ballets in the classical repertoire, and I also felt the weight of being one of the few Black women to take on the role.

By the time this performance came around, something shifted. I truly felt like I had nothing to lose. I had put in the work, found my voice, and discovered the artistic choices I wanted to bring to the role. That night, I was at ease and excited to step onstage. It wasn't just about the technique, though everything went as I'd hoped—it was about where I'd arrived mentally, emotionally, and artistically.

The performance felt like magic. I was completely present, fully connected to the character and the moment, and supported by an incredible network of people who believed in me. It remains one of the best performances of my career, not just because it went well, but because it reflected everything I had worked toward and overcome.

pas de deux prompt:
LIVING Each Day with intention

Life is like a dance—sometimes it's smooth and graceful; other times it's challenging and unpredictable. Each day is different, and that's what makes it exciting. We learn to be flexible, discover unexpected moments of joy, and get back up when we fall. While we can't control everything, we can set intentions for how we want to approach each day, focusing on the things that matter most to us.

Living with intention means thinking about what we can do to make each day meaningful. It's about taking small steps to grow, explore, and even help others along the way. It's not about being perfect—it's about learning, trying new things, and creating opportunities for yourself and those around you.

Your challenge: Reimagine Your Day

Take a moment to reflect on a day in your life—it could be an ordinary day, a fun and relaxing one, or even a challenging day. Write down what happened from start to finish. Now think about how you could enhance that day by adding a few intentional actions. What small changes could make it more joyful, meaningful, or inspiring? Let your imagination guide you as you reimagine your day!

Challenge yourself to add three of these:

Do an Act of Service: What's one small thing you could do to help someone else, and why would it matter?

Try Something New: What's one new activity or experience you could include, and how would it bring excitement or growth to your day?

Step Outside Your Comfort Zone: What's one uncomfortable thing you could try to help you grow or solve a challenge?

Do Something Creative: How could you add a creative activity, like drawing, writing, or making something, to bring joy or balance to your day?

Explore a Talent: What's one way you could work on a skill or talent you want to develop, and why is it important to you?

---

pas de Deux prompt:
what Does success mean to you?

Success can mean different things to different people. Take a moment to think about what success means to you. Is it reaching a goal, overcoming a challenge, or doing something that makes you happy and proud? Use these prompts to help you reflect:

- *My goal is . . .*

- *My challenge is . . .*
- *What I know about my goal/challenge is . . .*
- *What I've learned from my goal/challenge so far is . . .*
- *Some advice I've been given about this is . . .*
- *Advice that really makes sense to me is . . .*
- *My plan to achieve my goal/face my challenge is . . .*

As we reach the end of this book, I want to leave you with a few parting thoughts and something fun to try. If you're working toward a big dream, facing challenges, or just discovering what makes you *you*, remember that every step of your journey is important.

Pas de Deux Prompt: Picture Your Path

Before we close, here's one last challenge for you—it's all about dreaming big!

Take a piece of paper and imagine yourself ten years from now. What do you want to be doing? Who do you see yourself becoming? Draw or write about your future self and the life you want to create. Then think about one small step you can take today to get closer to that vision.

Remember, it doesn't have to be perfect—this is all about having fun and letting your imagination soar!

Dear Reader,

As you finish this book, I hope you're taking away more than just my stories and advice—I hope you feel inspired to write your own. Life is a journey filled with opportunities to learn, grow, and shine in your own unique way. No matter where you are right now, know this: You are enough, just as you are.

Throughout my career, I've faced challenges that could have stopped me in my tracks. But with the support of mentors, family, and friends—and by staying true to myself—I've learned to push through barriers and redefine what success means to me. Success isn't about living up to someone else's expectations; it's about finding what truly fulfills you, staying authentic, and creating a life that reflects your passions and purpose. My hope is that the experiences I've shared here help you discover your own strength, confidence, and path forward.

Whether you're chasing a big dream, navigating life's hurdles, or just figuring out who you are, remember this: You are capable of incredible things. Believe in yourself, stay curious, and don't be afraid to step out of your comfort zone. Challenges will come, but they're also opportunities to grow. And most importantly, know that your story, your journey, and your voice matter.

As you move forward, I hope you carry these words with you:

- Embrace who you are—every piece of your story makes you unique.
- Learn from your challenges—they're part of what makes you stronger.
- Keep dreaming big—because the world needs your light.

Thank you for taking this journey with me. Now it's your turn to take the lead and dance boldly into your future.

With love and encouragement,
Misty

ACKNOWLEDGMENTS

This book would not be possible without the love and support of my husband, Olu, and our son, Jackson. Your belief in me makes everything I do possible.

Thank you to my manager, Gilda Squire, for your unwavering guidance, and to my literary agent, Steve Troha, for your invaluable ideas and dedication.

A huge thank-you to my editor, Alyson Heller, for your meticulous care in shaping this book.

I'm deeply grateful to my coauthor, Nikki Shannon Smith, for your creativity and collaboration—this book wouldn't be the same without you.

A heartfelt thank-you to the talented illustrator Selena Barnes for your stunning cover art, which truly embodies the spirit of this book.

Finally, to all those who have supported me throughout my career, your encouragement has meant everything to me. This book is for the young people it's meant to empower, inspire, and uplift—just as you have done for me.

ABOUT THE AUTHOR

author photograph © 2025 by cregg pelman

Misty Copeland is a principal dancer at American Ballet Theatre and the *New York Times* bestselling author of *Life in Motion, Ballerina Body, Black Ballerinas, Bunheads,* and *Firebird.* She made her Broadway debut in 2015's *On the Town,* guest starring as Ivy Smith. Misty has been featured in the *New York Times* and on *CBS News Sunday Morning* and *60 Minutes.* She was named one of *Glamour* magazine's Women of the Year and *Time* magazine's 100 Most Influential People. Misty is the recipient of the Young, Gifted, & Black Honor at the Black Girls Rock! Awards and the Spingarn Medal, the NAACP's highest honor. Visit her at MistyCopeland.com.